on
nostalgia
by
david berry

COACH HOUSE BOOKS, TORONTO

Published with the generous assistance of the Canada Council for the Arts and the Ontario Arts Council. Coach House Books also gratefully acknowledges the support of the Government of Canada through the Canada Book Fund and the Government of Ontario through the Ontario Book Publishing Tax Credit.

LIBRARY AND ARCHIVES CANADA CATALOGUING IN PUBLICATION

Title: On nostalgia / David Berry.
Names: Berry, David (David M.), 1984- author.
Identifiers: Canadiana (print) 20200155253 | Canadiana (ebook) 20200155261 | ISBN 9781552454060 (softcover) | ISBN 9781770566231 (EPUB) | ISBN 9781770566330 (PDF)
Subjects: LCSH: Nostalgia.
Classification: LCC BF575.N6 B47 2020 | DDC 155.9—dc23

On Nostalgia is available as an ebook: ISBN 978 1 77056 623 1 (EPUB), ISBN 978 1 77056 633 0 (PDF).

Purchase of the print version of this book entitles you to a free digital copy. To claim your ebook of this title, please email sales@chbooks.com with proof of purchase. (Coach House Books reserves the right to terminate the free download offer at any time.)

For Nicki & Margot: Home

Introduction:
Play It Once Again

In the song 'Heaven,' David Byrne sings about paradise as a place where nothing ever happens. Though it is not really nothing – it's nothing new. The band here plays his favourite song over and over, at the same party, and it ends with a kiss that, when it ends, will start again, 'will not be any different / … will be exactly the same.' I don't believe there is much of anything after we die, but if there is anything like heaven, I am not sure how it could be anything but our greatest hits – maybe just our greatest hit – on infinite repeat. Everything else carries the potential for disappointment; we can't know what we will like the most, only what we *did* like the most.

As with most Talking Heads songs, this is not a straight-forward endorsement. There is a folk theory that the proper way to understand the album that 'Heaven' appears on, *Fear of Music,* is to add 'Fear of' to each of the song titles: the benign nouns then become the paranoiac's fear of cities, fear of air, and, thus, fear of heaven. This sense of unease creeps into the lyrics, too: Byrne repeats, 'It's hard to imagine / That nothing at all / Could be so exciting / Could be this much fun.' And of course the same perfect moment in perpetual loop is horrible: it's death. Quite literally, if you believe in this kind of heaven, but obviously in the metaphorical sense, too. Nothing is so definitive until there is no more of it.

'Heaven' – the song – happens to feature in one of my best memories, a fuzzy soundtrack to wee small hours hazily enraptured, utterly unaware of what came before and what was to come, a moment so obvious I did not take note of it; it just seeped its way into me and has never bled out. But I am not here to get lost in my own nostalgia, even if this little anecdote probably explains far more about why I would pick this particular song than my explanation will.

There is in 'Heaven' what I think of as the ultimate tension of nostalgia. It is a feeling that maybe feels too good, something that is so obviously appealing we can't help but be a little wary of it. We know it is severely limited, ending exactly when the kiss ends, leaving out every part before and after that either made it meaningful or cracked the moment. And yet no amount of rational defence can prevent it from returning, nor feeling every bit as right as it did the last time.

It's tempting here, for the sake of the parallel, to claim that it's hard to imagine how something so obviously blinkered and ultimately impossible could grab a hold of us, but it isn't, even a little bit. Our lives are a relentless push forward, and even if the path ahead is bright and brilliant, it will be littered with loss. Everything is fleeting, everything must pass, and the idea that we might every so often stop and look back and hope more than anything that we could have even the smallest part of it back seems as natural to me as the fact that we will never, ever be able to.

It's this duality that draws me to nostalgia, the impossibility and the inevitability, the fact it just keeps happening even though it can't. There is some sense now, I think, that nostalgia is a more prominent, more powerful force now than it has ever been. That is probably true. But surely the desire to go back has been and will be with us for as long as we go forward – surely there's a reason we made it possible to play the same song over again.

1

The Continuous Vibration of Animal Spirits: On the Why of Nostalgia

Nostalgia has an air of total irreconcilability. There is the feeling the word describes, of course: a fundamentally impossible yearning, a longing to go back even as we are driven ceaselessly forward, pushed further away from our desire even as we sit contemplating it. But it's the actual feeling, too, that ceaselessly resists any attempt to give it shape or sense. If we say we feel nostalgic, in general or about something in particular, it rarely needs an explanation, and there likely isn't a good one anyway: Why should it be the smell of our grandmother's cookies or the feel of a particular sweater or the sight of a certain tree in a certain playground, and not something else, that sends us searching backward? Why is it welling up now, on an otherwise unremarkable Tuesday? Why haven't I felt this way for a long time? Why does it matter? And that assumes it even occurs to us to interrogate this sudden rush: one of nostalgia's more persistent qualities is its ability to elide reason, to be felt deeply without prompting any further inquiry.

It's this strange aura of elusive profundity that makes nostalgia seem less like some sort of modern condition than a universal feeling that took us some time to put our finger on. If feelings in general are internal experiences that demand expression whether or not we have the means for it, our inability to actually do anything with nostalgia might be what kept it ineffable for so long. Most kinds of longing can be settled in one way or another, if not necessarily to the satisfaction of the yearner. Nostalgia can only be lived in or abandoned: it is yearning distilled to its essence, yearning not really for its own sake but because there is nothing else to be done. Maybe it resisted definition so long because naming it doesn't help resolve anything anyway.

Appropriately for the elusiveness of the concept, the word *nostalgia* did not originally mean what we now consider it to – also appropriately, it was coined with a longing for a time when there was no word for what it described. Specifically: in 1688, a Swiss medical student named Johannes Hofer gave the name *nostalgia* to a malady he had noticed in young Swiss people who had been sent abroad – chiefly mercenaries, one of Switzerland's prime exports at the time, though also household servants and others who found themselves in 'foreign regions.' As was the style at the time in the nascent field of 'medicine more complicated than bleeding humours,' Hofer used a portmanteau from an indistinctly highfalutin form of Ancient Greek: *nostos* roughly means 'home' – although it more often means 'homecoming,' which incidentally was also the name for an entire subcategory of Greek literature, most notably the *Odyssey* – while *algos* means, more simply, 'pain,' derived from Algea, the personifications of sorrow and grief, and a common classification at the time, attached to a variety of maladies that have since gotten either more precise or more vernacular names. (If you ever want to stoke excessive sympathy from, say, your boss, tell them you have cephalgia or myalgia – a headache or sore muscles, respectively).

So *nostalgia* literally means 'pain associated with home' – or, in slightly more familiar terms, 'homesickness.' This is not a coincidence, but more relevantly, it's also not a case of fancy medical-speak being dumbed down for popular consumption. At least not generally: the English word *homesickness* is a more or less direct translation of *nostalgia*. But the original term is French, *maladie du pays*, and not only does it specifically refer to the tendency of the Swiss to powerfully miss their home country, it precedes Hofer by at least thirty years. Hofer's coinage brought a specifically medical dimension, insomuch as medicine as we know it existed in his time: Hofer's observations were quite detailed, but still entirely anecdotal, and subject to a lot of conjecture. What he lacked in scientific rigour he made up for with linguistics, attempting to legitimize medicine's dominion over the concept with multiple coinages, including *nostomania* (obsession with home, which, as you'll see in a second, is probably more accurate to the 'disease' as he conceived it), *philopatridomania* (obsessive love of one's homeland), and, years later, in the second edition of his thesis, *pothopatridalgia* (pain from the longing for the home of one's fathers, which certainly has the advantage of precision, if not rhythm).

Though the difference between mere homesickness and medical nostalgia was mostly a case of ancient language, Hofer nevertheless describes a serious disease, one that could progress from simple physical ailments like ringing in the ears or indigestion to near-catatonia and even death. Its root cause, according to Hofer, was 'the quite continuous vibration of animal spirits through those fibres of the middle brain in which impressed traces of ideas of the fatherland still cling.' As Helmut Illbruck explains in his book *Nostalgia: Origins and Ends of an Unenlightened Disease*, essentially what that means is that the nostalgic suffers from a powerful obsession with their home that eventually makes them entirely insensate to any other experience or stimulation. Illbruck points out that the action Hofer describes does loosely capture how the brain seems to store, process, and recall memories – we'll get into that in a bit – which may explain some of why his concept caught on, at least in the medical circles in which it persisted for the next few hundred years.

As it happens, though, a primordial understanding of the structure of the mind isn't the only key insight that would stick to nostalgia even as its conception developed. There are two other big ones. First, Hofer recognized that nostalgia was less about whatever the nostalgic claimed to be missing than about 'the strength of the imagination alone': it seemed to have less to do with any material differences in the patient's circumstances than with the collective weight of their memories, even though those were centred on a very real and specific place. Hofer's final, curiously potent observation is his suggested cure, which he meant quite sincerely, but which elegantly captures the futility of trying to tame nostalgia, disease or otherwise: 'Nostalgia admits no remedy other than a return to the Homeland.' In all his observations and diagnoses, Hofer does not seem to fully appreciate that home is often more time than place. The proof of this will reveal itself as nostalgia evolves into something so incurable that it stops being a disease entirely, and its longing begins to be associated specifically with times past – but we are getting slightly ahead of ourselves.

Doctors proceeded to speculate about the causes of and potential cures for nostalgia until roughly the twentieth century, often ignoring Hofer's observation about the imagination's effects, causing some curious mutations in the idea. Nostalgia did remain almost the exclusive province of the Swiss for the first few hundred years after its naming – one of the original German words for homesickness, in fact, was *Schweizerkrankheit*, or 'the Swiss illness.' Hofer's near-contemporary Johann Jakob Scheuchzer – a Swiss naturalist who was chiefly interested in rescuing his countrymen's reputation from accusations of weakness – suggested that it was the change in air pressure (and maybe even quality) that made them so prone to debilitating longing. He suggested that a brief stay at the top of a tower or on a hill might restore some of their strength. There isn't much proof Scheuchzer's conception of the disease or cure ever really worked, but there is some indication that this sort of thinking is where Switzerland got its reputation as a healthful place to recover in a sanatorium or spa. Well after Scheuchzer, eighteenth-century physicians spent some time looking for a physical locus for nostalgia – a specific brain structure or bone – which was just as futile, with even less of an impact on Swiss tourism.

Gradually, the notion of nostalgia attached itself almost exclusively to soldiers – Swiss mercenaries being very popular hires in armies across the continent, and doctors being a regular part of army life. It would take a little more than two centuries for doctors to figure out that there might be something more than a mysterious nerve disorder causing young men whose sole job was dismembering other humans and dying gruesomely to yearn for the comforts of home; in the meantime, cures and coping methods grew a little more creative. There are stories, including one from Jean-Jacques Rousseau's *Dictionnaire de musique*, of foreign officers banning the playing of Swiss *ranz-des-vaches* – cow-based folk songs, historically played by herdsmen on horns as they drove their cattle down from the mountain pastures – and even the sound of cowbells, lest it paralyze their troops in nostalgic reverie. (It became a tenet of folk wisdom about the Swiss that the *ranz-des-vaches* had this power over them; it featured as metaphor or plot point in eighteenth- and nineteenth-century philosophical dialogues, dramas, poems, and operas, particularly by German Romantics, who were constitutionally interested in a disease that spoke so acutely to our conceptions of self.)

By the 1800s, the terrors of nostalgia finally spread to other countries' soldiers. Russian physicians recommended burying alive anyone who started showing symptoms, to stop the spread of the disease – which apparently did prove quite effective. On the other side of the Atlantic, the American Civil War saw several outbreaks among the young fighting men, even though they technically had never left their homeland, per se. Their physicians were a bit kinder, suggesting occasional removal from front-line fighting would bolster their spirits (not that the doctors didn't also suspect that the nostalgia betrayed a deep flaw in their character). The American army did apparently continue furtive explorations of the concept all the way up to the Second World War, chiefly as a way to reduce desertion, and nostalgia did maintain some interest for psychologists and psychiatrists in the first half of the twentieth century, albeit in a downgraded form: it became less disease than symptom or even disposition, usually of people who had far bigger and more immediate problems (a 1987 survey of its common historical-psychological invocations cited 'acute yearning for a union with the preoedipal mother, a saddening farewell to childhood, a defence against mourning, or a longing for a past forever lost'). Despite these last tendrils, the Civil War was really the last time anybody was diagnosed as a nostalgic, as such: nostalgia was largely abandoned by the medical community by the last decades of the nineteenth century. This seems to have had less to do with any particular breakthroughs regarding brain structure or mental health than with the general inability of anyone to make meaningful headway on understanding, let alone curing, nostalgia.

As it moved out of the medical realm and into the cultural, though, nostalgia did not fully shed its strange stigma. It first took hold in the worlds of philosophy and theory, albeit used interchangeably with the idea of homesickness, where it tended to be classed as a symptom of disorder – if not of the individual, then of the society they had built. Friedrich Nietzsche, in *The Birth of Tragedy*, is indicative of this line of thought: 'One is no longer home anywhere, so in the end one longs to be back where one can somehow *be* at home because it is the only place where one would wish to be at home.' From almost its earliest non-medical considerations, nostalgia was regarded as a kind of reaction to the modern condition, a port in the discombobulating and alien storm that was modern life. Philosophers, critics, and theorists are still exploring variations on this theme, though as an object of critical theory nostalgia has gradually lost any meaningful sense of place (or even, arguably, a time) and gotten more tightly entwined with the notion of authenticity and our search for the same (as such, its usefulness and meaning spiked slightly with the waxing and waning of postmodernist thought). This is what underlies something like Baudrillard's observation in *Simulacra and Simulation* that 'when the real is no longer what it used to be, nostalgia assumes its full meaning': the underlying implication is that if we were awash in some sense of the authentic, we would not have much occasion to look backward to find it – let alone yearn for a return.

It took some time for the popular conception to catch up to the cultural theorists. Homesickness as an idea percolated through the first half of the twentieth century, but it wasn't until the fifties and sixties that nostalgia, as both concept and preferred term for that concept, really started to insinuate itself into the popular consciousness. Like much about nostalgia, the precise reasons for its sudden surge in popularity are fuzzy and elusive: Fred Davis, in his 1979 study of contemporary nostalgia, noted that even in the fifties *nostalgia* had been considered a 'fancy word,' limited to professionals and 'cultivated lay speakers,' but by the sixties it was in common enough parlance to be the subject of consideration in popular books and magazines. One theory Davis alludes to is that, as the notion of 'home' became less potent – as people moved around more frequently, gained easier access to increasingly widespread sources of information, and became less creatures of a specific place – *homesick* lost some of its power, and *nostalgia* slipped in as a way to capture the same feeling without being tied down: essentially, *nostalgia* became a better metaphor for the feeling it was trying to describe. The concept of home became a time, not a place, so we needed a new word for it.

This seems entirely plausible: to modern ears (and even at its coining), *nostalgia* is itself a nostalgic word, an evocation of some more glorious past, a time when they knew how to name these feelings, if not actually deal with them. You can see some evidence of this in the way nostalgia was popularly defined in the time before we had dictionaries in our pockets: broadly. Its hint of classical, distant authority allowed writers to indulge some poetry, misdefining it in ways that nevertheless captured the ethereal import of the subject: a generic 'overwhelming yearning' or the 'tragic pain of loss.' (The TV series *Mad Men*, set in the sixties, captures this perfectly when its central character, Don Draper, claims *nostalgia* is Greek for 'the pain from an old wound.') Windbag Chicago mayor Richard J. Daley was purported to have told a crowd at the ribbon-cutting of some major project in the sixties that he was 'looking to the future with nostalgia,' which either suggests that the word was widely understood enough that he thought he could be clever or – more probably, based on Daley's reputation – that it was widely known but still vaguely understood as a kind of longing.

Even if people were fuzzy on the exact Greek roots, nostalgia as a concept was solidified in the popular consciousness by the time of Davis's book: he neatly summed it up in his title, *Yearning for Yesterday*. It was a strong enough force that Davis openly wonders if the seventies represented some kind of peak in nostalgic feeling. Though he himself admits that this would be impossible to measure and that nostalgia was probably universal anyway, he makes a compelling case that the seventies was at least a boom time for open use of the term: 'nostalgia shops,' a sort of midpoint between antique stores and thrift stores, were a staple of retail streets; book clubs and sports memorabilia suppliers openly branded themselves with 'nostalgia' in their names; there was even a periodical, *Liberty*, whose tag line was 'The Nostalgia Magazine' and that consisted solely of reprinted articles from its original run, which had ended in the early forties.

If the word *nostalgia* is no longer novel enough to be used as branding, its presence in our collective consciousness has certainly not diminished any since Davis's day. If we complain about Hollywood strip-mining our nostalgia for an easy buck, or if we post pictures of nineties toys under a hashtag, everyone knows roughly what we're talking about. We don't even really need to conjecture here: nostalgia is ubiquitous enough to have been repeatedly studied by psychologists around the world, and their findings confirm that we all think the word means roughly the same thing. The largest study, pulling in more than 1,800 students from seventeen culturally and geographically diverse countries, found that people associate nostalgia primarily with memories and the past, and that these memories are almost all fond ones. Underneath this surface understanding, nostalgia generally provokes a certain sense of happiness, but for almost everyone it is strongly tinted with a sense of longing or loss – and often, of course, a desire to return. If asked, most of us basically define nostalgia as bittersweet memory.

Even that, though, is not precisely accurate: the tastes aren't properly mixed, except in retrospect. They are more shot and chaser than one large gulp. Nostalgia is sweet, finding its undertones of bitterness only when we become aware again that it is about our memories – snapshots of a time we can never relive, outlines of a home that has been wiped from the map. It's this aspect that gives nostalgia both its mystery and its meaning: why on earth should we feel this way? What part of our humanity demands that we should be not just drawn toward our past but pulled so hard that it pains us? Why is this phenomenon so important that we had to rehabilitate a disorder just so that we might adequately express it?

However much we like to claim that it's a modern condition or the sole province of the wilfully deluded, there is every evidence that nostalgia is indeed a universal part of the human condition: a setting to be toggled, not a trait that can be picked up or discarded. Eckart Frahm, professor of Assyriology at Yale, estimates that nostalgic writings started showing up about two hundred years after Sumerians developed a codified language – just enough time for sufficiently old records to accumulate that people might start feeling like their own time was missing something. And that's only nostalgia on a societal scale: as we'll explore in more depth in Chapter 3, art is littered with nostalgic feeling from its earliest days – it was prevalent enough to make up a whole subcategory of Greek storytelling, after all. And being aware enough of the feeling to name it has done nothing to diminish its prevalence: another batch of psychological studies found that roughly three-quarters of people feel nostalgic at least once a week. They're the median of a population that leans heavily toward nostalgia: more than a quarter of people reported feeling nostalgic at least three to four times a week, while only 4 percent claimed it happened less than once a month.

What is it, though, that sends us yearning backward? Often as not, it is simply interaction with something from our past: sometimes that is as simple as the smell or taste of a madeleine, though slightly more often it is the presence of another person – many nostalgic memories are centred on family, friends, and other significant people in our life, although that probably has more to do with how we value social connections than with some underlying quirk of our memory. This is understandable but feels a little inadequate: of course we will remember things, but why should we yearn for them when we know we can't ever get them back? The answer might lie in what actually appears to be the most common trigger for nostalgia: feeling bad.

It would be wonderful to have some grander explanation, but here we are. In terms of the spectrum of bad feelings, loneliness seems to be the most common trigger, but really any sort of vaguely baddish mood will do, from anger or feeling threatened right on down to simple boredom. (Perhaps I shouldn't sell boredom short: psychologist Clay Routledge theorizes that it might prime nostalgia because bored people are tapping into the grander existential angst that comes from lacking purpose.) The basic idea is that by casting our thoughts backward to a time when we weren't feeling bad, we find some comfort, or maybe more importantly some steel, to help us carry on. To use loneliness as our example, it seems that when we're feeling isolated, we have a reflex to think back to fine times with friends and family, reminding ourselves that we have been surrounded by love and companionship before and presumably will be again. We are, in effect, turning our past into our present – even giving ourselves a tenable future – by reminding ourselves that we are still that person who was not so lonely, not so long ago.

As far as we can trust the psychologists, their findings are a curious reversal of nostalgia's origins. In labelling it a disease, Hofer assumed nostalgia was the cause of its subjects' physical maladies and psychological distresses, when, even then, it was the result of them. People felt bad and so longed for the last time they felt good – which, given the limits of sixteenth-century life, was almost inevitably the last time they were at home; their problem wasn't necessarily that they were away from home, just that they were currently miserable. The psychologists' conception of nostalgia does fit in quite nicely with several of the reigning theories of nostalgia from more contemporary figures, though: the postmodernist search for authenticity tracks, for instance, if we're to assume that lacking authenticity would leave us in some sense distressed. In mildly less airy terms, Davis – who was by trade a sociologist, and included anecdotal but deep interviews in his studies – theorizes that nostalgia works as a way of helping us consolidate our identity, and we are especially prone to it when that sense of identity is under threat. There may be a bit of a chicken-and-egg question with regard to threatened identity or diminished authenticity and feeling shitty, but either way the outcome would presumably be the same: nostalgia as a balm, a way to get us back on our feet.

Whichever level we are considering it on, the fact that nostalgia is as much coping mechanism as reflexive condition might help explain why modern nostalgia, despite having shed its diseased origins, is often treated dismissively or with suspicion. Nostalgia can be a fairly benign reaction – a warm memory at the smell of freshly baked cookies – but just as often it might be properly understood as a sign of distress: a lonely, depressed person flailing about for their last notions of happiness. That is slightly overstating things: by most accounts, nostalgia is a fleeting experience, a few short moments or maybe a night of reminiscing among friends. It works its restorative or melancholy magic and moves on. But that's all the more reason why someone or something who seems pervasively nostalgic might make us uncomfortable:

somewhere deep down, we know they are trying to cope with some void of meaning or motivation, and it's easier for us to mock the crutch and keep our distance than to confront their despair and risk having it provoke a similar void in ourselves. Or perhaps it burrows down even deeper than that. Maybe the mere existence of a pervasive and inescapable tendency to fling ourselves into the comforts of our past is a general reminder that meaning and identity are more elusive than we are willing to admit, hard to grasp and harder to hold on to, and so we have plenty of reason to feel disconnected from our very selves, without even getting into the rest of humanity.

In fairness here, it's not just impending existential crisis that leaves us uneasy with our tendency toward nostalgia (though that's probably the way I would vote). Even among those who defend nostalgia, even as a coping mechanism, there is a pervasive sense that, whatever nostalgia's benefits, it involves an inherently blinkered view of our own past. Nostalgia is in a real sense dishonest – if not actively, then in that slipperier lie-by-omission way, not really giving us the whole truth about what came before. This is a more solid charge, if only for the fact that almost everyone is nostalgic about their past, even if those pasts strike us as objectively horrible: people who lived smack in the middle of the Depression, the Blitz of London, rampant civil unrest, meaningful threat of nuclear war, repressive police states – almost anything up to genocide (depending which side you were on) – will often describe those times in glowing terms, or at least pluck the tiniest shard of rose-coloured glass from the ashes and let it redeem the rest ('Sure we were starving, but people stuck together back then'). Davis found nostalgic recollection inherently dishonest; he noted that most of his subjects at some point engaged in what he called 'reflexive nostalgia,' wherein they openly questioned their own nostalgic recollections – usually immediately after sharing them. He didn't seem to fully appreciate how the presence of an accomplished sociologist openly probing them might affect how people try to be perceived: relatively few sessions of reminiscence, with or without other people, end with us disavowing the whole thing as BS to make ourselves feel better. (Davis also detailed a further layer of nostalgia, interpreted nostalgia, which he described as analytical questions about nostalgia – 'Why am I feeling nostalgic now? What is the purpose of nostalgia?' – which I can say from personal experience is profoundly rare among people who are not actively researching nostalgia or being questioned by people who are actively researching nostalgia.)

Regardless of how reflexive we ourselves might be, we are acutely aware of how warped other people's nostalgia often is. This is not without cause: if anything, we are probably not nearly suspicious enough of how inadequate our memories really are. The most common demonstration of our faulty recollections is flashbulb memories, the tendency people have to vividly remember major events while also somehow getting virtually all of the details wrong. The most studied event in relation to this phenomenon is 9/11; there have been at least two dozen studies of people's memories of that event and how they have changed since. In these and related studies, researchers will talk to people relatively soon after an event, having them record what they were doing; the researchers will then return after a year or two or five or ten, and ask them to share the story again. Almost inevitably, the stories have changed dramatically – but the rememberers are so sure of their current version of events that they tend to accuse the researchers of lying, right down to forging handwriting or faking voice recordings. Their memories are not just supplanted, they are supplanted with impossibly vivid but wildly inaccurate ones – at least outside the basic facts of planes hitting buildings and the like.

Though they are generally attached to significant collective experiences, flashbulb memories are not so different from anything we would call a memory. For almost anything to stick in our head for any length of time, there has to be a reasonably strong emotional experience attached to it. Partly this is because the more apparently meaningful an experience is, the more we will return to it, and that repetition, the frequent firing of neurological pathways, is important to storing memory. (This is the sense in which Hofer was generally right about how the mind forms memories, and in particular why memories that are frequently revisited will be so vivid they might seem to block out more recent experiences.) But it appears that powerfully emotional experiences will also retroactively enhance memories, bringing what had appeared to be background information to the fore. If one of your co-workers unexpectedly asks you out, for instance, that experience will cause related things that might have escaped your notice before to seem more vivid: you will remember an awkward elevator ride, or a compliment in a meeting, that had previously faded into the background hum of life. It's an idea that rings true if you attempt to plumb your memory – try to vividly recall a specific day's commute from three years ago, or eating an average sandwich. Outside of the things we don't generally consider memories – reflexive, rote stuff like riding a bike or tying a shoe – there really isn't any such thing as an unemotional memory.

In and of itself, this would be a biasing factor for our past: our memory is all extremes. We are naturally going to forget the humdrum, and even for that matter the mildly to majorly unpleasant or the only somewhat exciting. Barring the most traumatic experiences, which force their recollection on us, we are likely biased toward generally pleasant memories, too, as we'll tend to replay those more often. But as the flashbulb memories demonstrate so clearly, it increasingly appears that not only do we plainly forget a lot of our experience, but we profoundly alter what is left. Recent research by the likes of Karim Nader and others, in fact, seems to suggest not only that we have the potential to alter our memories almost every time we recall them, but that it might actually be impossible for us to recall something without altering it in some way. The brain, far from remaining fixed, apparently returns to something like the original state it was in the first time the memory was recorded, with the potential to be subtly rewritten if it's given the appropriate cues: say, another person sharing their experience on 9/11, or maybe, as has been attempted with PTSD patients with some success, a therapist helping throttle the emotions associated with the memory. It's akin to walking across a snowy field: the first time you do so, you create an obvious path. The next day, the wind has covered it with a light dusting: the outline may be obvious, but because your balance is a bit shakier or you're walking with a friend or you're looking at your phone, you can never quite replicate the exact steps. Walk it enough, with enough tiny shifts, and the path ends up in an entirely different place, but still looks, from the end, like the same one you started with.

Considering all this, you'd be absolutely right to accuse nostalgics of yearning for a past that isn't there. Between our need for reassurance and our tendency to subtly and (mostly) unwittingly alter our most meaningful memories – which is to say, virtually all of them – we are left with a feedback loop that would gradually but persistently turn our own past into a perfect shining gem, precisely the memory we need to get us back on our feet and out in the world, regardless of its relationship to what 'actually' happened. But mistrusting our nostalgic tendency in this case seems entirely beside the point. Left to ourselves, we have no meaningful way to separate our basic, unyearned-for memories from the rose-coloured memories we associate with nostalgia; limited by its mechanics and our need to maintain a coherent, motivated self, our memory inherently creates a past where everything is deeply meaningful. Not necessarily pleasant or perfect, mind you, but sufficiently comforting that we can turn to it whenever we need (which is at least once a week, for most of us). Our memory is built for nostalgia: it may not force us to yearn to go back to the experience, but given the choice between the abject chaos of our present and a reasonably ideal past – presented to us as our actual past – nostalgic longing hardly needs the help.

And that, of course, is only if we are left to our own devices, which hasn't really been the case since we invented external media. Whether you want to mark the starting line at cave drawings or would prefer to wait until we managed to put together entire systems of writing capable of clearly explaining complex ideas, making records of our worldly concerns – from the particulars of goat trading to the inner-most thoughts of **~~iceprincezz420~~** – is such a profound thing that we may not be entirely capable of handling it.

Whatever myriad tasks we might currently use our multi-media cornucopia for, memory is the essential spark of media – the why and what of it. Wherever it pops up, the first things we try to write down are all those that presumably mean disaster if we were to forget them: the oldest instances of systemized Chinese characters we have, for instance, are inscriptions on oracle bones, literal attempts to divine the actions of the gods (some people also think some cave paintings served divination purposes, if you want to go back even further). The original Sumerian cuneiform tablets, probably the first thing humans did that could properly be called writing, were basically accounting ledgers, tracking the commerce and contracts necessary to keep a city of thousands fed and not feeling excessively homicidal toward one another. However our blinkered memories muddled through before, we eventually reached a point where an external, verifiable source was needed, and so we created it.

Whatever its uses for the collective, though, the invention of media creates two pretty serious problems for the individual that are particularly relevant to nostalgia: fallibility and mutability. By creating a history that transcends us, we reveal not only that our understanding of things – our memories – might not really be true but that our understanding of ourselves may not be as solid as we would like to think. Of these problems, the extent to which we misremember things is the more obvious: we may not be entirely incapable of recognizing our own failings without an external prod (or proof), but having one certainly has a way of focusing the issue, if only because it makes it harder to deny that we might be wrong. The reaction of the subjects of the flashbulb memory study is some proof of how profoundly uncomfortable this dissonance is for us.

But the internal dissonance that external memory – media – provokes is ultimately more troubling. The great lie of our self-identity is its consistency: we are effectively trapped in a permanent presentism, a belief that we are fundamentally the same, enhanced and emboldened by a memory that selectively edits our past to conform with that notion. The external record enabled by media reveals that there are times when we felt differently, when we experienced the world differently. Whether through an express record of our feelings (say, a diary or a piece of art we've created) or just an external nudge that forces us to re-experience our feelings, rather than merely live with the memory of them (say, watching a favourite movie from childhood), we are forced to confront the fact that we change, that we are less solid than our necessarily solipsistic movement through the world would have us believe.

In both of these cases, external media reveals our boundaries, how limited in our understanding of the world we truly are. Nostalgia is, I think, one of the most powerful tools we have developed to help us reconcile those boundaries. Though it's a phenomenon that exists well beyond external media, it is thoroughly enhanced by it, in the sense that nostalgia is a powerful coping mechanism. Media does not create the longing, it creates a real past; nostalgia is what allows us to reconcile it to our present, to give it meaning and allow ourselves to carry on.

In the sense that nostalgia is a modern condition, it is only because the modern age is so thoroughly mediated – increasingly, it seems, with every generation. Illiterate peasants might go their entire lives without being forced to square these particular circles; an endlessly wired world, one where even most social interaction is inescapably mediated, will be forced to confront it endlessly. A world awash in media is a constant test of our memory – and as such a constant test of who we are, or in any case think ourselves to be. Confronted with evidence that there is more to the world – more to our self – than how we feel and experience it in this moment, we scramble to find firmer footing, to reconcile how we feel with the way things are. Trapped as we are in ourselves, this solidity is only ever available in retrospect – and because it is impossible, all we can do is long for it. Nostalgia is a form of reconciliation: not just of who we were with who we are, but with the idea that that either of those questions has a settled answer. It helps us believe we might be more than just this longing.

2

Spineless Admiration:
On Anti-Nostalgia

Though the conception of nostalgia as a disease, or even just a symptom of a troubled mind, faded away in the early part of the twentieth century, the popular understanding of nostalgia hasn't entirely shed the hostility that usually attends disorders of the mind (or body). Nostalgia is frequently regarded with a certain pointed suspicion.

If you do not quite clock this tendency in the world at large, it is glaringly obvious in the way most academics who have studied it in psychological, sociological, artistic, and historical terms tend to write their introductions: nearly all take particular care to try to justify nostalgia, not just as a subject of inquiry but as a worthy, necessary, or at least overall helpful part of the human condition. Many of them positively reek with the nervous sweat of an author worried about being branded as some kind of misty-eyed sentimentalist reactionary, and even the calmer ones tend to take as a given the fact that most readers' initial response to the subject is going to be negative. (This, in fairness, probably says as much about the culture of academia as it says about any background distaste for nostalgia.)

If the cloisters tend to concentrate it, though, more casual discussions of nostalgia often share the same buzzing background apprehension. This is evident in how often calling something 'nostalgic' or accusing someone of indulging in nostalgia is used as a sort of general slur, an easy shorthand that suggests some level of moral failure or backward thinking without much further explanation needed. This is the kind of nostalgia evoked when someone complains about Hollywood's latest slate of revivals and reboots, or accuses teenagers of appropriating fashion trends from before their birth, or in slightly more serious cases snipes at a political opponent. This usage of *nostalgia* is rarely very specific: it can suggest that the target is anything from a sentimental patsy too easily seduced by saccharine stories or things that prop up their own ego, to someone who is generally naive or misunderstands history, to the kind of rock-ribbed reactionary who won't rest until every pair of pants comes with suspender buttons by default. Its prevalence and its imprecision make the point, though: people rarely seem to have a coherent explanation for why the nostalgia might be bad; it's just nostalgia, so it's bad.

Before we dive more deeply into the ways nostalgia manifests itself in our society, it's worth pausing to consider this discomfort a little more pointedly. Whether it's an appropriate reaction or not is up to the reader, but in any case I think it's an essential aspect of the modern experience of nostalgia, a lingering guilt or unease that tends to colour our experience of it, even if we have fully swallowed all these arguments that it's a mostly benign, restorative force that helps give our lives meaning.

In any event, beyond its nebulous negativity, the overarching unifier of this sort of casual denigration of nostalgia is that it is almost universally applied to other people's nostalgia. Our own nostalgia might be restorative, or interesting, or might just flit by without sparking further reflection, but other people's nostalgia is a mark of some deep failing. This complaint – whether it exemplifies the usual dissonance between positive and negative traits (he's cheap where I'm thrifty; she's pushy while I'm assertive; they're blinded by nostalgia, whereas I'm merely nostalgic) or comes from those unique types who rarely feel nostalgia but see it everywhere – is not a sustainable critique. In the vast majority of cases, people who are speaking against nostalgia have a very specific instance of it in mind, and to whatever degree *nostalgia*-as-insult does capture some of nostalgia's darker dimensions, there is an extent to which it is just the most convenient term to lob at something you don't especially like anyway.

Which is not to say we shouldn't be suspicious of our tendency toward nostalgia, nor even that a healthy degree of skepticism isn't the most appropriate course of action when nostalgia flares up in ourselves or others. Nostalgia has some plainly essential functions to our identity, even if we only conceive of it as a restorative, but as the lady says, the difference between medicine and poison is dosage.

On that metaphor, overindulgence in nostalgia is likely the most clear and present danger: it is certainly the aspect of nostalgia that seems to provoke the most hand-wringing, although the fact that the growing and excessive prevalence of nostalgia has been a recurring theme since the time the concept entered the general discourse suggests either that we are in a rearward-facing death spiral or that critics of nostalgia might also want to start complaining about our general lack of self-awareness. (Maybe both.) Nevertheless, the point stands: in the same way that a healthy fantasy life is helpful – for distraction, for goal-setting, just for fun – but tattooing the name of your Hogwarts house on your forehead and embarking on a mission to kill Voldemort demands drugs and therapy, the case against nostalgia begins where restraint ends. The precise location of that line is again both nebulous and easier to spot in other people, but the downfalls are glaringly obvious, all curling off the root problem that the fulfillment of nostalgia is inherently impossible. In effect, overindulging nostalgia is living in a dream world, albeit one that's made more enticing and intoxicating because it comes with the sheen of historical plausibility. Occasional yearning for that dream world may be understandable, but actually trying to return to it is only to allow the world that's in front of you to crumble from neglect; as with all escapism, the almost inevitable reinforcement – things are bad, you retreat to the past, things get worse, your buffed-up past starts to look even better – only makes it more dangerous.

A prescription against excessive nostalgia can often be a bit of a hedge, though: too much of anything can be a bad thing, and anyway, much of what is true of really indulging nostalgia is arguably true of any amount of nostalgic feeling. Nostalgia – or, more precisely, the specific history that nostalgia prizes and yearns to return to – is inherently untruthful, its fundamental yearning unfulfillable; it is dreamy and impossible even in its most fitful spurts. Even if it performs some essential function for our identity or well-being, it may be better for us to try to find those benefits in something more tangible or truthful; alcohol is a powerful stress release, but exercise is probably better, in the long term.

The essential problem with throwing out nostalgia, though – hence the prevalence of the hedge – is that to do so almost inevitably ends up throwing out history, too. This is at least partially because, as noted in the first chapter, there is often considerably less daylight between nostalgia and history than we might like to think. But it is also because there really seems to be virtually no way to maintain a history without provoking nostalgia: again, the very act of recording and disseminating the past is what appears to lay the groundwork for our wistful remembrances of it. Which is not to say that people don't try to do away with the entire project.

We don't need to look terribly far to see this in action: though our own era is routinely derided for its supposed prevalence of nostalgia, the advocates of dismissing the past are also doing quite well. Chief among these are what you might consider modern Panglossians, a group of thinkers and critics who are resolutely convinced that the current era is the best of all possible times. As a group, these people share one primary trait: times really are quite good for them specifically. They tend to be pretty firmly ensconced in some upper echelon of the current world order, one of your captains of industry, 'public intellectuals,' handmaidens to political power, etc. This perch has convinced them not just that the world is fundamentally just and meritocratic – why else would they be where they are if everyone didn't get what they deserve? – but that any kind of looking back, especially with longing for what came before, is not just pointless but some kind of moral failing.

The most prominent of these is Steven Pinker, who has made what must surely be the most lucrative career (outside the self-help industry) of convincing people that everything is fine and they are the problem. In books like *The Better Angels of Our Nature* and *Enlightenment Now*, he argues that, owing to a variety of broad-stroke, global improvements to things like frequency of violence and poverty rates, we are sitting at the apotheosis of human culture, a rocket ride that will end only if we give up on the lessons of the Enlightenment. Human life, at least for the past few hundred years, has been nothing but progress, and so any desire to change its current path – or even just stop and take stock of where we are – is a way of gumming up the moral arc of the universe. (It perhaps goes without saying that the Panglossians also tend to believe that the key to a prosperous future is to just keep doing what we're doing right now, which can lead them to make weird pronouncements like 'We're at the end of history' and such.)

For all this surface present-boosterism, though, Pinker and his ilk's actual view of the past is often just as rosy and ill-formed as that of the most histrionically nostalgic: though they would certainly never advocate a yearning for what came before, their central idea that our recent cultural history is a relentless and undeniable advancement overlooks both how much happenstance has been necessary to get where we are and how precarious and illusory their notion of this apparent peak really is (being able to choose an arbitrary endpoint makes it extremely easy to cast vast societal forces in your preferred light).

If this type of anti-nostalgic feeling is relatively easy to sweep aside, though, it has roots in more fundamental challenges to the notion of nostalgia. The idea of steady and essentially irreversible progress, for instance, is central to the precepts of the scientific method, in which our knowledge about the physical world is very much like the metaphorical tree, spreading and branching from a solid core that grows and strengthens with the overall breadth. We do need to be careful of taking this way of thinking too far. For starters, as I think the Panglossians demonstrate, scientific methods, much less scientific knowledge, don't always withstand the chaos of human culture particularly well. The scientific method is not religion: it is a way of exploring one aspect of our world, not the way for doing everything. And, of course, scientific consensus has been frequently proven wrong, whether because it has chased a concept down a blind alley or because it has made grander pronouncements than our current understanding can support.

But the point is that the scientific method is an inherently progressive system, one that, theoretically at least, must build off all the knowledge that came before (even the parts that are ultimately misguided). In a system like this, history is essential, but nostalgia is practically nonsensical: even to yearn to go backward would effectively be to give up the entire project, to return to a place of wilful ignorance and enforced stasis. (Hence the reason the ethical dilemmas of science typically revolve around whether we should use some bit of knowledge we have acquired: cut off too many branches and the tree might die.)

Whatever the practical limitations, it's not hard to extend that ethos to ourselves. To what extent aging can be defined as progress in the positive sense of the word depends on the person, but our identities, what we understand ourselves to be, are inherently progressive: we are the sum of what we have done, experiences piling on top of each other like wet clay. Some kind of deep knowledge of those things, of our personal history, is essential to knowing what we are.

Returning to those times, though, besides being impossible, would also seem to effectively stop the whole business of living, cryogenically preserving some iteration of yourself without even the promise of thawing it out. And that's only the yearning aspect of nostalgia: the overall effect our nostalgic tendencies have on our memories, lessening if not eliminating some aspects while promoting others to core experiences, would seem to doom the entire attempt to know ourselves, leaving us like some floating consciousness grasping at flotsam and trying to claim that as our authentic selves. (Which is more or less exactly what's happening, but that doesn't mean we shouldn't try to fight it.)

This can all seem like a freshman philosophy concern, but this general sense of unease does trickle down into our lives quite frequently. Anyone who has ever tried to argue that they don't have regrets – or that you shouldn't have them, either – is effectively endorsing the same basic conception of identity, even if they're trying to downplay the bad instead of emphasizing the good; the point is that everything you've ever experienced all adds up to where you are now. A more forward-thinking endorsement of relentless progress, and often a more explicit thrust against nostalgia, can be found in the current corporate culture of Silicon Valley, with its tenets of fast and frequent failure and #hustle. (Which, for all its typographic innovation, is just the dominant permutation of what you might call American Dream capitalism, in which you are less what you came from than what you're obviously going to be, at least until it's time to write a memoir.) Here the past is often little but a story of inevitable becoming, something to be used as anecdote or proof of moxie, but certainly not a time for which to yearn.

Silicon Valley culture also has ties to another force that is arrayed against nostalgia: its most frequent moral justification is that it's building a technological utopia. Utopians are not always quite as purposefully forgetful as Silicon Valley, which at times seems to want to blank-slate the world and replace it all with something that involves an algorithm, but in its purest form, utopian thinking is quite close to a nostalgia for the future – nostalgia's polar opposite, at least along the axis of orientation to time. Here, yearning for the past is replaced by a kind of fanatic eagerness for what's to come; given our experience of time, utopia is technically possible, which should be an important distinction. Though, of course, even avowed utopians would generally admit that their paradise is more of a direction than a realistic goal. (I am obliged by law to note that the original word as conceived by Thomas More was a pun on the Greek words for 'good place' and 'no place.') So it's probably fair to say that utopianism and nostalgia are equally frustrated longings, and this fundamental impossibility is essential to the experience. Still, the impossibility of utopia is a spur to action. If the dominant negative image of the nostalgic is of someone frozen in a rosy amber, thwarted by glory they can never reclaim, the worst that can be said about the equally starry-eyed utopian is that they are too much a dreamer, and will have to be more practical. Ultimately, the promise of utopia is the only kind of yearning that any progressive system can swallow wholeheartedly, which makes it a natural antipode for nostalgia.

For the most part, this inexorably progressive mindset is not openly hostile to nostalgia so much as it has a philosophical predisposition against it, a general unease with the concept that anyone might think things were better before, despite all that progress. (To the extent that we live in a world where progress is a basic value, then, pervasive if low-grade hostility for nostalgia is pretty self-explanatory.) Still, for more specific attacks against nostalgia, we have to look to programs that have chosen progression as an ideal, not made it their engine. One of the prime examples of this can be found in the avant-garde, the loosely connected but definable series of cascading artistic movements that dominated the visual arts – and heavily influenced most other art forms – for most of the twentieth century (and arguably even through today). In their quest to constantly redefine art, avant-gardists inevitably arrayed themselves very explicitly against what came before, including the idea of longing for and even recreating the standards of earlier eras, often taking on nostalgia even before it had become codified and widespread.

Since its conception, the term *avant-garde* has tended to be watered down to mean anything that is consciously unique, so it's probably important to set our boundaries a bit here. In his landmark critical work *The Theory of the Avant-Garde*, Italian theorist Renato Poggioli makes the case for the avant-garde as a distinct school with a handful of underlying philosophies. One of the key misconceptions he addresses is that there has always been an 'avant-garde,' when in fact it's a distinctly modern tradition, 'born only when art began to contemplate itself from a historical viewpoint,' according to Poggioli's compatriot Massimo Bontempelli, one of the progenitors of magical realism in fiction. Without getting too into the weeds of art history, the essential insight here is that, though there have frequently, even constantly, been new styles of art, the underlying formal goals and theories remained fundamentally similar, what we might call classical values. If we can limit ourselves to painting, for instance, though there's an undeniable difference from the flat frescoes of medieval churches to the lush, vivid works of the Renaissance or of Rembrandt, any sense of newness really comes from technique and, later on, subject. The ultimate goal – which, if I'm going to be brutally simplistic here, is the realistic depiction of a scene for glory of god, humanity, or at least the painter – remains unchanged. To put it in the terms of the most common way of discussing art these days, for most of human history, no one would have looked at the absolute freshest canvas of the most renowned painter and been confused about whether it was even art, let alone insisted their kid could have done it: all art seemed like art because it all flowed from the same principles.

In contrast, the avant-garde's goal is effectively newness: newness not just of what's depicted or how, but of what one might even consider art, or ways to create art – of the very values that inform the questions the artist is trying to answer. Challenging the notion of what constitutes art is a good enough shorthand for what an avant-gardist does, although in many cases that challenge is merely the starting point for a more fulsome assault on ways of seeing, speaking, and even being. But again, the crucial distinction here is that the newness is not merely happenstance or the natural consequence of some other change: it is actively sought. Though this is common enough now to seem the natural state of things – or at least arty things – that perception is more a sign of just how deep into our bones avant-garde thinking has sunk. As American art historian Bernard Berenson noted, 'The lust for otherness, for newness, which seems the most natural and matter-of-course thing in the world, is neither ancient nor universal. Prehistoric races are credited with having so little of it that a change in artifacts is assumed to be a change in populations, one following the other.'

As it happens, the modern preconditions that make the soil ripe for avant-gardism are quite similar to the ones that encourage nostalgia, too. For starters, both are immensely aided by a certain romantic individualism, the idea that your specific experience and identity are worthy of attention and cultivation. More profoundly, just as a nostalgia that extends beyond personal experience requires an exposure to mass medias capable of recording and widely disseminating history, avant-gardism requires an acute historical knowledge; the former demands you know what it is you're missing, where the latter needs to know precisely what it is throwing away. If, as is frequently assumed, the modern condition is one that is inevitably alienating, leaving us desperately thirsty for a sense of meaning and self but lost in a sea of potential meanings, none of which readily present themselves as the Right Choice, nostalgia and avant-gardism are essentially opposite responses to the sense of unease that follows: nostalgia reaches backward toward the last available font of meaning, whereas the avant-garde embraces the sense of discombobulation by making that its ultimate goal. Floating in space, nostalgia tries to ground itself where avant-gardism tries to fly.

Poggioli traces this tendency back as far as the baroque period, *baroque* as a term having roots in concepts like flaws, the bizarre, and the needlessly complex – all things that suggest a strong break with traditional notions of aesthetic beauty. Though it also pops up in a number of Romantic- and Gothic-adjacent movements, avant-gardism likely has its purest expression of ideals with the Italian Futurists of the early 1900s, who crystallized a lot of notions of why and how art must be made different – and whose style of loudly broadcast manifestos, furious reimagining of every aspect of society, and insistence on novelty became something of a template for artistic movements for most of the rest of the twentieth century.

The Futurists, led by poet and theorist Filippo Tommaso Marinetti, claimed they were spurred to action by the relentless industrial modernity they found around themselves in Italy in the first decade of the 1900s. In his *Manifesto del Futurismo* (you'll never guess what it is in English), Marinetti praises things like roaring racing cars, 'good factory slime,' 'movements of aggression, feverish sleeplessness, the double march, the perilous leap, the slap and the blow with the fist,' and the beauty inherent in struggle. The Futurists' modern world was one of speed, muck, and violence – the latter two of which they would get plenty of when they enthusiastically supported the First World War – but nearly as important as what they were praising was what they were decrying: nearly anything that even catalogued the past, let alone glorified it in any form. Marinetti promised that the Futurists would 'deliver Italy from its gangrene of professors, archaeologists, tourist guides and antiquaries,' comparing museums, libraries, and academies to cemeteries – adequate for the dead, invalids, and prisoners, but useless to vigorous young men such as himself. He even hoped that his contemporary Futurists would be discarded by younger, stronger, and more modern men – inevitably men – when they reached the decrepit age of forty (an opinion that seemed to change by the time he hit that age). From Marinetti's spark, a veritable flood of manifestos followed, all particularly obsessed with destroying the past: the *Manifesto of Futurist Painters* claimed they were rebelling against 'the spineless admiration for old canvases, old statues, and old objects,' while the architecture wing claimed that every generation would have to make its own city anew, with people outliving their own houses.

Though the past in general was the most common target of Futurist ire, Marinetti himself did occasionally single out nostalgia as a disease, most acutely in his later manifesto, *We Abjure Our Symbolist Masters, the Last Lovers of the Moon.* The title is a reference to his second futurist manifesto, *Let's Murder the Moonlight!*, and that exhortation would become something of a mantra for avant-garde artists of all stripes, whether they were pouring it into manifestos or not: avant-gardists love ripping apart the popular art of the generation that preceded them. Specifically, Marinetti was aiming at symbolist poets like Poe and Baudelaire, and his specific complaints were that they were a bunch of foggy-headed sentimentalists in love with the past. 'For them,' he writes, 'no poetry could exist without nostalgia, without the evocation of dead ages, without the fog of history and legend.' He goes on to propose replacing the 'sickly, nostalgic poetry of distance and memory' with a 'poetry of feverish expectation.' In practice, this meant disregarding syntax and varying his typography to supposedly capture the immediacy of his very modern emotions – though from where I sit, it seems like Marinetti's true art was flame-throwing theories of how art should be. In any case, like most critics of nostalgia, Marinetti did not really pause to explicate it, assuming that people would fairly clearly understand both what it was (gazing longingly at the past, even going so far as to actively keep it alive) and why it was bad (because everything about the past was bad).

Whatever Marinetti and his Futurist contemporaries' particular peccadilloes – one of them would turn out to be actively aligning themselves with Fascism, but more about that in a second – their general attitude formed the philosophical underpinning for the consciously avant-garde, or at least actively transgressive, in both niche and popular artistic movements for the next century or so. Futurism's most immediate relatives, from the Surrealists and Dadaists in the visual arts to the Modernists in poetry, made an explicit point of decrying their immediate forebears – if not dismissing them as entirely illegitimate, then at least suggesting their work did not fit with a radically new age – and doing away with the past in an attempt to redefine what their art forms even were, frequently producing works that classically trained or just marginally older audiences and critics sometimes failed to even recognize as work. This became such a pronounced tendency in the visual arts that its recent history is essentially a cascading array of prominent movements that switch up aesthetics but hold on to the main idea that the role of art is to challenge the nature of art: abstract expression gives way to pop art, which accedes to performance and site-specific work, which is confronted by digital mediums, and so on. But the basic tendency shows up even in more popular and more actively commercial mediums, too: postmodern literature isn't quite either, although it has the same tendencies, but in any case, things like the rotating cast of national New Wave cinemas and successive waves of guitar-based rock music – punk, metal, hardcore, grunge – all share the basic structure of actively tearing down the past, erasing any desire to hold on or return to it, for the express purpose of attempting to define an entirely new present.

While considerably less deliberate, this ethos has also filtered out more generally into a mode of pop-cultural consumption that is obsessed with the new or novel, from cultural gatekeepers crowning semi-annual emerging trends in independent music and film to the perpetual tabloid obsession with eternally young pop and movie stars, each grabbing a moment of spotlight before being replaced with the newest version. One could argue that the very model of pop music – to say nothing of fashion, video games, and online influencer culture – is explicitly anti-historical if only incidentally anti-nostalgic, concerned primarily with the new and different, in facade if not in any meaningful substance. Some of this might just be the natural failings of people versus their art: 'This Charming Man' will never get bloated and disconcertingly nativist, but Morrissey has, so we need to discard him to make room for someone who scratches our itch for a literate, doomed romantic of ambiguous sexuality. It's more than that, though: the fact that a pop star who can pull off even a decade of sustained attention and chart success is enough to qualify as a world-bestriding legend whose legacy is beyond repute – a Beyoncé, a Taylor Swift, a Rihanna – is some indication that a certain relentless freshness is one of the driving forces of the genre. Really, though it's fashionable to decry the constant retro obsessions of our pop-cultural landscape, these might stick out so sorely precisely because the enduring hum of modern culture is the endless churn, the discarding and forgetting of the old and foregrounding of new young things that Marinetti yearned for. Whereas before the past and our desire for it was an oppressive force that needed to be actively dismantled, now it is more like a wrench in the gears of our progress, noticeable precisely because the machine is supposed to be running without it.

Whether it is the dominant mode of culture or not, the point is that an articulated notion of progress that is explicitly anti-nostalgic has existed for more than a century and has successfully permeated even the parts of our culture for whom *manifesto* is just an edgy name for a fragrance, not something to publish dozens of as a form of self-justification. Still, while it is the most robust and successful case against nostalgia ever made, even it has a tendency to fall back into nostalgia, and not just when the various movements' founders get old enough to miss when they were the hot newness.

In fact, as often as not, nostalgia is baked into the very core of these purportedly radical, avant-garde ideas; it just happens to be a nostalgia for a time well before whatever it is they are reacting to. For Marinetti and the Futurists, the decrepit, cemeterial past was primarily the celebrated Italy of the Renaissance, which of course was in deep thrall to the glories of antiquity. If they were all too happy to burn the museums of classical art, though, they were enthralled by what they considered to be primitive or even primordial art, whether it was in the racist exoticization of African and Indigenous arts or reaching back to the paintings and sculptures of cavemen, and incorporated some of the forms and techniques into their painting and poetry. They occasionally even went so far as to call themselves 'the new Primitives,' which underlines the rather expansive historical knowledge you need to start declaring history useless and also that yearning for a blank slate might be the most atomic form of nostalgia humanity indulges. These inherent roots to their project were further exposed through their association with Fascism, which Marinetti enthusiastically pursued. If the initial sympathies between the two movements had to do with an embrace of industrial modernity and a thirst for violence, Fascism's more practical need to produce a nationalist identity that people could rally around eventually led it to embrace Italian history with a fervour that even its predecessors, who created the actual Italian state, could not match. They recognized that forming something truly without precedent is, if not entirely impossible, hard enough that the vast majority of people will find it incomprehensible; as ever, the real future is made by selectively editing the past, not discarding it entirely. Whatever Marinetti would have thought of this project in his youth – and contemporary critics, most notably Giuseppe Prezzolini, in his essay 'Fascism and Futurism,' expressly laid out the obvious contradictions between the two movements – by the time Mussolini was in power, Marinetti replaced his lust for the new and his desire to be expunged in his dotage with prime patronage appointments in academies whose express purpose was the preservation and promotion of Italian national identity through art. That he got to pick what mattered seems to be the only conviction that stuck with him.

Though other avant-garde movements do not have hypocrisy exposed so plainly, they are trapped by the same contradiction, and even when they are aware of it, they can't fully escape it. The other major branch of Futurism, the Russian Futurists, who shaped so much of early Soviet culture, started as a gaggle of primitivists, primarily interested in the idyllic, pastoral Russia. Though they proclaimed an 'insurmountable hatred for the language existing before them' and were swept up in the Marxist revolutionary fervour – utopian

Marxists are considerably more natural bedfellows for avowed futurists than the Fascists were – all their works survive in the same Russian they decried, and many of their aesthetics drew on the same primitive forms that interested their Italian brethren. The so-called primitive forms pop up again and again in visual art movements, though when it comes to nostalgic yearnings, the medium hardly matters: Modernist English poets decried the formalism of the Victorians while actively harkening back to classical times, and punk tore apart the increasingly expansive landscape of rock by returning to the three-chord simplicity of blues. As often as not, creating something revolutionarily new simply means finding a different set of reference points than the ones used by whatever is currently dominant: artists try to escape the past by going further into it.

Ultimately, it is this inescapability that really fuels our discomfort with nostalgia. Things that are handily discarded are no source of anguish; it's only when we seem to need them that we start to feel anxious about them. In the same way that prescriptions against sentimentality are expressions of our discomfort with the fact that human connection – love – is an inescapable urge, so too is our hand-wringing about nostalgia the product of some dim awareness that it is fundamental to our experience. So long as we remember, so long as we have history, we will be drawn toward it, as illogical and impossible as that may be. Forces of that nature are rare and terrifying; if they should not necessarily be feared, they should absolutely be respected. The only way to approach power is with a healthy skepticism.

3

I'm Just So Tired of All These *Star Wars*:
On Art and Nostalgia

There is usually a level of solipsism or arrogance in the assumption that art shapes the world: if you are the type of person to make art, or just consume significant quantities of art, then naturally your point of view and the world it's looking out on are going to be pretty thoroughly influenced by the collection of artistic interpretations you're soaking in. But an economist will tell you the same thing about incentives and rational actors and what have you. Rationally, we're all going to have plenty of incentive to devote our lives to the things that make the most sense to us, or at least to assign outsize importance to the thing we've devoted our lives to. We decide what makes the world.

When it comes to the mess of our internal lives, though, the competing morass of urges, emotions, and rationalizations is, if not completely defined, thoroughly shaped by art. We could go so far as to say that one of the big, overarching purposes of art is to grasp at the unnameable maelstrom inside us, either to name it ourselves or to borrow the label that someone else has been kind enough to extract. Knowing ourselves is a task both elusive and illusory – if you'll forgive the cynicism – so we turn to an array of options that seem to have figured something out to give ourselves half a shot at it.

The experience of nostalgia is, naturally, almost entirely defined by art, at least in the practical realities of day-to-day life. Psychological studies into the matter don't go back much more than thirty years – and, with apologies to the psychologists, do not seem to factor into the understanding of nostalgic experience for anyone who is not currently employed writing about the subject. Pathological study, however misguided, is a little better than three hundred years old – and, with all due respect to early doctors, about as useful to our general understanding of the issue as bloodletting is to curing depression. Well before we had a useful name for nostalgia, though – well before we even had related concepts, like homesickness – artists were exploring this fundamental drive we feel to go back, the yearning to reclaim what we once had. Now, in fairness, most of the classical sources of nostalgic longing were pretty explicitly tied to actual places, to home in its physically manifested sense. Odysseus's journey – one of the founts of the term *nostalgia*, if not quite of all nostalgic art – is decidedly more rollicking than most brooding odes to homeland lost, but it nevertheless captures the underlying desperation of the longing to return. Ovid's *Tristia* and *Epistulae ex Ponto* – written in his exile from Rome and with a not entirely undeserved reputation as whiny emo garbage – certainly capture the overwhelming despair of being forced to move along, and the ways in which the impossibility of return can poison the soul if it's dwelled on too long. Contemporary travel was not easy enough for Homer or Ovid to realize that home is more time than place, but the longing is still fundamentally the same, and anyway, their sentiments were real and relevant enough to speak to people throughout and across centuries.

Even with more specific and rigorous methods available to us, art still tends to dominate how we think about nostalgia and what we mean when we say it. Naturally, the big change from the classics' grasping for literal homelands is the clear distinction that nostalgia is about time, the past to which we can never return, the place of which only memories remain. This does tend to muddy the waters a little. Though people can define it more sharply if they're ever actually forced to think about it, quite a few tend to regard nostalgia as primarily Proustian: memories, in this case overwhelmingly warm ones, sparked by an encounter with some meaningful object from one's past. If we want to be strict about it, *À la recherche du temps perdu* explores, by Proust's own telling, involuntary memory in general, the feeling of being sent off into a reverie, helpless to stop it. This experience certainly can be nostalgic, and maybe even primarily is, but the nut of nostalgia is really the longing, not merely the recollection – the fact that seeing that cassette tape or tasting that madeleine does not just take you back, but in some sense makes you want to go back. This might not be a useful distinction, though, and not just because fuzzy internal experiences like nostalgia are only ever going to be what we can agree they are: the natural, involuntary process of memory-editing is only going to leave us with meaningful, primarily positive memories to begin with, on top of which the line between yearning to return to a time and simply being content to live in a pleasant memory for a while is not at all clear, even to the person experiencing this pull backward (and even if they're not exploring that experience for seven volumes).

Still, there is a reason that – at this point in time, anyway – the Proustian automatic evocation feels inadequate. An involuntary nostalgia seems more suited to a time when the past was actually harder to come by, when we required the right baked good or building or, god forbid, person to thrust us back into the past. Our era is one that is littered with relics, one that preserves the past in any number of explicit and happenstance ways. We are not just more often exposed to the past than an asthmatic Frenchman who would have had to put his hands on a physical copy of any book he wanted to read; we are often able to seek it out, to comb through an archive of personally meaningful objects until we spark the exact nostalgic experience we were after.

Modern nostalgia is probably best captured by the likes of *Ready Player One*, a novel and later a film in which the combined infinitudes of human imagination and perfectly immersive virtual reality allow the characters to live in the pop culture of the 1980s until society collapses. Here nostalgia is entirely voluntary, a well we dip into whenever we feel like it (although it feels more like a compulsion). As a result, the sources are far broader. It's not necessarily about personal experience; it's about feeling a kinship with an identifiable time. Of course, the writer of the book, Ernest Cline, was just splaying out his own childhood interests, but the story is actually set in the 2040s, with its teenaged protagonist obsessed with an era he missed by a couple generations.

We don't blink at this promiscuity toward meaningful pasts now, but even as recently as 1979, sociologist Fred Davis did not regard yearning for a time you'd never lived in as proper nostalgia; he thought of it as pure fantasy, like yearning to live in the Alpha Centauri system. Certain online corners have termed this tendency 'anemoia,' although it doesn't seem to be distinct enough from what we understand nostalgia to be to catch on. The more expansive contemporary definition of *nostalgia* probably makes more sense, anyway: given the fungible nature of our memories, there isn't as big a gap as we might like between what we believe we have lived through and what we know only through second-hand account and reference. And besides, the borders of time are also more porous than we want to allow, and eras have a strange way of daisy-chaining through the ages: if in two decades' time some *Ready Player One* fan buys a framed copy of the movie's 1980s-style poster, which era is the fan really evincing nostalgia for? If my Christmas tradition involves watching a digital stream of *Scrooge* – a 1951 film, based on an 1843 novella, that I watched on VHS in the 1990s because my parents grew up watching it on TV in the 1960s – how do we meaningfully separate the layers of first-hand longing and second-hand nostalgia?

Beyond being a fun philosophical exercise, the more fundamentally transformative aspect of this sort of grasping at nostalgia is that it attempts to bleed some of the impossibility out of the concept: you can't really go back to a mythic 1980s – or 1920s France, or Ancient Rome, or whatever – or even the real childhood experiences of interacting with all this culture for the first time, but if you surround yourself with it, constantly relive it, well, aren't you going back, kind of? Nostalgia here is not just a mere feeling, haphazardly accessed, but a full-on way of being.

Ready Player One also points to another modern quirk of nostalgic experience, namely just how much of a role art plays not just in our basic understanding of nostalgia but in the actual tangible realities of it, too. It's relevant that popular culture is the underlying language of *Ready Player One*'s nostalgia: in both book and movie, certain personal touchpoints are threaded through the story – an unrequited romance, a childhood bedroom – but even these are almost all framed by some form of pop-cultural artifact, whether a particular video game puzzle or, at one point, literal recreation of a movie's dialogue, word for word. This was not always the case: again, Davis speaks of nostalgia as primarily centred on personal experiences, and even more contemporary theorists of nostalgia like Svetlana Boym tend to overlook nostalgic attachment to art and media figures. (Although, to Davis's credit, he recognized how rapidly these cultural figures were crowding onto the scene and, even more astutely, how easily they could be exploited by the media companies that controlled their likenesses and could make money from their memory.) From a place where the referencing and outright revival of prominent pieces of pop culture seem to make up the majority of our collective interaction with nostalgia, it almost seems like we're discussing different concepts entirely. The yearning for yesterday is still prevalent, though; it's just been colonized.

Before we go on, it might be helpful here to nail down what exactly we mean by art and popular culture. This is not a distinction I'm particularly fond of making, but in the case of nostalgia it does actually seem to have some relevance to how they are perceived. Keeping it broad enough to be palatable, and trying to be descriptive rather than prescriptive, I would argue art is any creative output, unbound from the limits of factuality, that seeks to interpret the world through the framework of a particular medium – anything from cave painting and interpretive dance to video games and, of course, books. Popular culture is a subset of art that tends to carry a lot of baggage, positive and negative, but is essentially just art that shows its scaffolding a bit more, chiefly because it has been produced more recently. Things like its intended audience and message, economic realities, and the gradual evolution of style are much more obvious and present in the work; we're explicitly aware of the context of its creation, mainly because we are part of the context of its creation. Obviously this is not a perfect distinction: *Police Academy* and *Paris, Texas* both came out in 1984, and probably neither has ever been considered anything other than pop culture or art, respectively. More obscure contemporary arts, like dance or sculpture, aren't ever really considered popular culture, although that's more because most people are just ignorant of their context. For the purposes of popular discussion, though, this tends to be a reasonably descriptive definition: pop culture is art we haven't got around to admitting is art yet. I suppose if you wanted to be a little more snotty about this, you could call the distinction art that's dead versus art that's still alive, although again the meaningful divide is probably art that has proven its worth to be called art by virtue of some vague notion of cultural import, and art that we are still unsure of, art that might be worthless detritus but might actually be real art. (If you are going to insist mere pop culture isn't art, or even worse that it is simply entertainment, I cannot help you and, in the latter case, am frankly surprised you have even managed to read this far.)

For the most part, though, the distinction is not all that important. Pieces of art in any subcategory are a natural breeding ground for nostalgia, especially but not only if they're getting a capitalist's assist. On the most fundamental level, it's because they are experiences that shape us as much as any other: in the same way that, say, a road trip with friends can feel foundational to who you are as a person, a book or film can be crucial to forming your point of view, who it is you believe you are. If anything, art has the advantage of being both experience *and* object, the thing that shapes you and its own reminder of that experience, too. It's tempting to say that art is even also its own memory of that experience, though that's not quite right: to some degree, the nostalgia that individual pieces of art evoke in us is for the experience of first encountering them, of first dealing with something that rewires our internal machinery. This is a necessarily reductive idea of our personal connection with art: ideally, maybe even inevitably, revisiting some beloved song or painting or movie will create some new experience, will interact with our changing self to reveal something else about both the art and us. But even this minimal understanding of what art means to us is fertile for nostalgia: anything that reveals ourselves to ourselves will be a prime locus for longing, and arguably this discovery of new depths is simply a side effect of being inspired enough to attempt to return. If a small cake can make us feel nostalgic, it stands to reason that the book in which we read the cake anecdote would be capable of something equally powerful.

This feeling is only enhanced by the fact that art often works as a kind of social glue, too, something that binds us together and defines us in larger groups. Considerable chunks of our social lives are given over to some kind of combined artistic appreciation, whether it's just informally discussing whatever came out on Netflix that weekend or a months-in-the-making group trip to see that band you love at that cool festival in California. Entire social subcategories are defined by what kind of music people listen to or whether they're willing to watch films with subtitles; art is a bonding experience, a way for a group to know itself as much as an individual, and so is often the subject of broad, collective exercises of nostalgia. These might even be more powerful than our individual connections to any piece of art, given how essential it is for us to feel like a part of something: witness how often the death of some pop star or writer will occasion sentiment along the lines of 'They taught me it was okay to be weird' or what have you. Art is now a tribal totem, an essential tool for coming together.

But even then, we don't necessarily need to feel a strong connection to some piece of art for it to prime some nostalgic longing in us. Artists' intentions are a breeding ground for accidents of interpretation, and some of the most powerfully nostalgic aspects of art are happenstance. Some of this is pure chance, of course – a film's character happens to be wearing the exact same scarf as your ex, or the scene is shot outside the café you happened to visit while you were in Paris. (Film is almost certainly the medium most likely to spring these accidents upon us, and I would not be the first to suggest that, as an accidental record of things like fashions, settings, and sounds, it is the most fundamentally nostalgic medium, full of potential sparks of yearning.) And then there's the fact that art is often very specifically trying to evoke a certain time or place: it's not universally true, but art is often a pretty clear record of some kind, whether by virtue of having been created in that time or being specifically created to evoke that time. This is not necessarily the deepest level of nostalgic connection, but it's a good bet that our frame of reference for any particular time period is as formed by art that depicts it as by any history book or plain photograph, and it seems natural that interacting with this kind of art would on occasion make us yearn for that time. Whether it's wanting to sip whisky with the suits in *Mad Men* or wander around Joyce's Dublin, art creates times we can long for, and helps us fill in plenty of reasons to start longing for them, whether borrowed from the piece or created on our own.

All these flavours of nostalgic experience make art a potent source of it, but they also have the tendency to confuse the issue somewhat when we try to talk about what role nostalgia plays in art. Not that we generally seem aware of this confusion: *nostalgia* is a word that tends to get applied to art without much further consideration, though really ambitious critics and commentators might take the time to point out that it was coined by a Swiss doctor in the seventeenth century, or even that it used to be considered a disease. Most just assume everyone gets it. And yet even which mode of nostalgia we might be specifically referring to – are we talking about some important childhood memory getting a reboot, or just the fact something is making the eighties seem cool again? – is glossed over, the term applied equally to revivals, reboots, sequels, prequels, retirement tours, reunion tours, and absolutely anything that even touches on some earlier era, from full-on proper English period dramas to high school movies that take place before smart phones.

Even these drive-by invocations usually have some point: nostalgia is often some part of a particular artwork's appeal to an audience. The thornier issue is that so much of our consideration of nostalgia and art rests entirely on the level of audience appeal and how that might inspire artists (or at least their funders) – we assume that mere nostalgia is driving the popularity or even the creation of these things. This kind of assumption rests on such a heaping pile of other inherent assumptions about the purpose and parameters of art that it rather easily collapses into incoherence at the tiniest tug.

This is usually clearest when we look back at pieces of popular culture that are old enough to have slipped out of the usual churn-und-drang of everyday attention, where the immediate context of their supposed appeal has somewhat melted away, and we're instead interacting with them on the more opaque level of because they're there. Consider something like *Back to the Future*: leaving aside any nostalgia for the film itself – *Ready Player One* rather prominently features a version of its famous DeLorean, for example – it could putatively be considered as something of a cash-in on 1950s nostalgia. It has some classic hallmarks of what folk wisdom considers blatant nostalgic traits, namely its setting – thirty years earlier than its 1985 release. Though some argue that the nostalgia cycle is closer to twenty years – and maybe even speeding up – this interval is presumed to be roughly the amount of time it takes for youth to grow into people with enough clout to make major works of art devoted to their nostalgic recollections, or with enough money that they can dictate the output of capitalistic producers. You might also argue that it depicts things as basically all right, the quintessential small-town American life of sock hops and entirely imaginary racial harmony. (As has been pointed out frequently, *Back to the Future*'s weird racial inversions are probably the most delusional, if not really properly nostalgic, thing about it: Marty McFly ends up not only inspiring a Black soda jerk to run for mayor but inventing rock and roll, to the delight of the all-Black band playing the Enchantment Under the Sea dance.)

And yet, the incidental thrills of seeing classic cars or a guy wearing 3-D glasses as a fashion statement aside, *Back to the Future* is as anti-nostalgic as a film set in the past can be. (There's some indication that even the studio's marketing department was aware of this: it was mostly pitched to 1980s teens as a blockbuster romp.) Early on in the film, Marty McFly's mother recounts, with a degree of romance, how she and his father came to meet – and this is almost immediately revealed to be bullshit as soon as Marty makes it back to 1955. He finds out that his father has not only always been a coward who can't stand up to town bully Biff, he was also a pervert who met his mom because he fell out of a tree while spying on her changing. Speaking of his mom, she tries to seduce him, which I suppose you could maybe torture into some kind of parental nostalgia for being young and sexed-up, if you wanted to toss aside the whole incest angle. But then later she is almost raped, so. Marty is nearly bullied himself but manages to turn the tables on Biff by skateboarding, literally escaping how miserable the past was with a technique from the future. Desperate to get back home the entire film, he discovers when he finally succeeds that he has managed to make the present better by changing the past, effectively improving it – hardly a suggestion that we should be yearning for the past. Calling a film like this nostalgic – which still happened a lot during thirtieth-anniversary celebrations of the movie – is at the very least to misread much of what it is actually saying.

Audiences, of course, do misread things. But even if a chance to glimpse the 1950s on screen is what was driving people to see it – even if it's still what's driving people to see it – that doesn't particularly mean much for the art itself. Describing something's fundamental appeal as nostalgic feels like a way to pretend you've fundamentally engaged with it and have developed a thoughtful opinion. In the world of art and pop culture, chalking something up to nostalgia can too often be a dodge, a highfalutin way to say that something doesn't appeal to you and that you're not really able to get over that fact (or the fact that people make things not specifically designed to appeal to you).

The ultimate futility of this line of thinking is laid bare in the modern phenomenon of franchises, what in corporate-speak is intellectual property but what the rest of us are going to have to realize, at some point, is just culture, in the process of being made. The shining example of this is *Star Wars*, the poster boy for modern cultural production's obsession with remaking or otherwise expanding on what came before, instead of just hunkering down to make something new. *Star Wars* is a trickier case because it is, on several levels, very explicitly working in nostalgic modes – or in any case, the first film, which was retroactively named *A New Hope* when they decided to start making sequels, was. Set in a science-fiction context, it nevertheless announces itself as happening 'a long time ago' – though, more pointedly, the world of the film itself is littered with nostalgic references to glorious things that came before, incredible wars and valiant republics and nearly mythical laser-sword-wielding knights. The world of the film – if not broke down, used, and dusty – often looks like the remnants of something that was once glorious. Meta-textually, it is also nakedly nostalgic, aping the techniques of the movie serials and sci-fi flicks that George Lucas grew up on. Its story of clear good and evil could arguably be considered a throwback to childhood nostalgia, too, although that seems more obfuscatory than helpful – it's probably more accurate to just say it's simplistic.

Born from nostalgia, the series has since moved on thematically. Even if we limit it to the twelve theatrically released films, perhaps only one – *The Force Awakens*, which kicked off the newest trilogy in the universe's main storyline – deals explicitly with themes of nostalgia: its main antagonist, Kylo Ren, self-consciously apes the style of Darth Vader, while its faceless villains, the First Order, are openly reverent of the original evil empire, seeking to re-establish it as a force in the galaxy. That everyone openly nostalgic is also plainly evil could perhaps be a sign that the film doesn't have any warm feelings on the subject, although *The Force Awakens* almost perfectly mirrors the plot points of *A New Hope*, making that a somewhat trickier case to build. In any case, though all the later films are highly reverential and referential to the original trilogy, they branch off into other, equally simplistic themes, and manage to not just be twentyish hours of standing around talking about how cool it was when the first Death Star exploded.

The way we talk about *Star Wars* has not developed quite so much. Since the announcement of the first prequel series in the late 1990s – a massive cultural event that introduced the term *prequel* to wider culture – the reigning assumption has been that *Star Wars* fans are motivated by nothing so much as nostalgia, trying to recapture the thrill of when they first saw the movies as children and then went off to make lightsaber battle noises with their mouths. As is often the case, this isn't entirely without merit: fans who lined up for the prequels were generally pretty open about how much the series had meant to them as kids, and what it meant for them to have a chance to dive back into that world. When those same fans were deeply disappointed by the new movies – you can't go to Tatooine again – they were equally explicit that the experience went beyond disappointment and seemed to have destroyed a meaningful part of who they were: the prequels also popularized the charming phrase '[such-and-such] raped my childhood,' which was what fans on message boards and in songs claimed George Lucas was doing by making mediocre follow-ups. (There are now fairly significant communities that look back on the prequels fondly: people who were children when they came out.)

It's not just the prequels either. The eighth film in the main saga, *The Last Jedi*, pretty plainly tries to dismiss any warm-and-fuzzy feelings you might have about its predecessors: 'Let the past die. Kill it if you have to,' the now-conflicted Kylo Ren tells hero Rey, after she has already heard about what a useless bunch the Jedi were from previous hero Luke Skywalker. As of December 2019, the film has the lowest audience rating of any *Star Wars* movie on Rotten Tomatoes; it led to boycotts of *Solo*, the next *Star Wars* film to be released; and it is still inspiring twenty-minute YouTube videos about how much it sucked. All this negativity prompted its sequel, *The Rise of Skywalker*, to more or less directly disavow it, diving headlong into more of *The Force Awakens*' nostalgic recreations, to the detriment of narrative coherence but to the benefit of audience approval ratings. (Critics, for whatever it's worth, loved *The Last Jedi*.) All of this also takes place in the context of the fact that, for all intents and purposes, George Lucas himself spent much of his career as a nostalgia merchant: besides *Star Wars*, almost all of his major works as a writer, director, and producer are suffused with nostalgic tendencies, from the love letter to California car cruising, *American Graffiti*, to the adventure-serial revivalist *Indiana Jones* movies. (Although, complicating flip side: he also pioneered or heavily supported a lot of groundbreaking movie special effects, particularly CGI.)

So nostalgia is undoubtedly still part of the appeal of the *Star Wars* properties. But it's mildly tricky to talk about *Star Wars* as being something of the past or, anyway, something you would need to yearn to get back to. Even before the prequels, there was an entire 'expanded universe' – yet another term we can thank the series for – including dozens of novels and video games, some amusement park rides, and a few radio series, to say nothing of the reams of fan fiction, both published online and played out with the ample toys and licenced merchandise. Since the prequels, it's gone even further: there are now nearly four hundred novels set in the *Star Wars* universe, more than seventy video games, at least six completed or announced television series, and a handful of other animated and live-action movies. And, of course, since at least 1982, there have been legally obtainable home-movie versions of any of these films, in a variety of formats, that you could watch at your leisure. At a certain point, this franchise, or even just the films, are not really a reminder of the past, they are just the culture we live in – part of what surrounds us, penetrates us, binds us, if you will. (Sorry.)

Star Wars is an admittedly extreme example by virtue of its corporate-mandated ubiquity, but this is one of the fundamentally strange aspects of the interaction of art and nostalgia: at some point, our interaction with them ceases to be nostalgia and just becomes an intrinsic part of the world.

Things stop being pop culture and just become art, and our interaction with art rarely gets credited to nostalgia. No one accuses summertime Shakespeare festivals of rosy nostalgia for a bygone era – he is just our greatest writer, some essential part of the human condition. Reading him, performing him, appreciating him – these are not a yearning to return to the time of rule by divine right and women being banned from the stage; they are just participation in culture. Notions of canon or absolutely essential works are a little less popular than they once were, but nonetheless anyone who declared that they were purposefully going to avoid any piece of art made before right this second – or, I don't know, the moment of their birth – would be dismissed as a trivial philistine. This stuff does plainly serve as a sort of cache of cultural identity, the collected works by which we can know who we are and where we came from, and yet to talk about it in terms of nostalgia feels almost nonsensical.

Perhaps it's just the ravages of time: once things pass from our living cultural memory, it's maybe just less obvious to us that nostalgia plays a role in revisiting them. As discussed, though, we evidently do now consider nostalgia for times well before we were alive to be a legitimate kind of nostalgia, so that can't entirely be it. (Although philosophical inconstancy is rarely the worst explanation for human behaviour.) This is not a phenomenon entirely limited to the world of art and culture either: the line between yearning for the past and ensuring you know it, between nostalgia and memory, is fuzzy. But there is also something deeper to this strange divide than perhaps we're consciously aware of, and we can see it in one of messiest ways nostalgia interacts with the creation of art.

In his 2010 book, *Retromania*, Simon Reynolds explores the various ways in which a love for 'retro' is taking over popular music. Reynolds's use of *retro* is not much different from what might be considered a working definition of *nostalgia*: he defines it as a particular interest in the recent past, 'stuff that happened in recent memory,' though he suggests that people aren't really idealizing or sentimentalizing this past, but being charmed by it, making it a 'plaything.' (I'm not sure how much practical daylight there is between sentimentalizing something and merely being charmed by it, since people rarely reach back to play with the parts of the past they don't care for, but no matter.) He details a convincing list of rear-action movements in pop, including band reunions, album reissues, bands reuniting to play live versions of old albums, and the growing cult of the anniversary celebration, none of which have dissipated in the intervening decade.

Where his argument gets trickier, though, is when he gets into the tangled web of influence. Reynolds rightly points to a wave of pop and rock bands that seem to be obsessively cribbing from the past. As opposed to earlier artists, who strove for the new and relentlessly pushed boundaries – Reynolds cites in particular musicians of the sixties and the punk era – artists now seemed content to just mix together the sounds of the past; maybe they're searching out more esoteric influences, but still, their influences are fundamentally backward-looking, not pushing the limits of music further. He cites musicians like Ariel Pink, who defined his sound as a 'retrolicious' mix of his favourite sixties and seventies genres; Fleet Foxes, which updated seventies AM radio gold; and Vampire Weekend, which at the time was heavily praised for dabbling in the pop-does-Afrobeat vein of musicians like Paul Simon and Talking Heads. This isn't strictly meant as a denigration: he admits to liking all the bands. It just seems like a draining of pop music's previous vitality, its push for the new.

Reynolds's is the most cogent critique along these lines, but it's a common sentiment, especially in the youth-obsessed world of pop music, where fashion disguising itself as a sense of progression tends to dominate critical discussion. It is a weirdly self-defeating, almost mimetic critique in that it seems to indulge in a certain nostalgia itself, yearning for the perceived values of a different era; and just like much nostalgia, it requires a degree of amnesia about how art tends to be made. As much as we like to praise artists for originality and creativity, there is not a one of them who isn't simply a sum of their influences. Collecting, assessing, and recombining the things that came before to create something that feels fresh and relevant and unique to the time is more or less all there is to art, and the degree to which we can see the stitches is more often dependent on our own experience (or age…) than anything the artist is doing. Unless of course postmoderny stitch-revealing is one of the modes the artist is borrowing.

Jonathan Lethem illustrates this tendency rather brilliantly in his 2008 essay 'The Ecstasy of Influence: A Plagiarism': it's a meditation on how artists borrow and repurpose ideas in which every sentence is lifted directly from some other published source, with minimal editing for clarity. It's the starkest example, but we could as easily just survey any popular artist's career. The Beatles, the standard-bearers for sixties pop experimentalism, undeniably did some groundbreaking things with new studio production techniques – as similarly innovative as experiments with modern digital production, from Auto-Tune to sequencing programs – but they were still a gang of Liverpudlians who started off imitating the fifties rock and R&B records they grew up listening to, and much of their experimentation was just borrowing from art forms that were until then non-traditional influences for pop, from sitars to sound collages. This doesn't take away from their genius; it is the basis of it – John Lennon himself said about music, 'There are only a few notes. Just variations on a theme.'

Perhaps the issue is not so much the borrowing; it's that the reach is less broad than long. Perhaps there's something more worthy, artistically or morally, in selecting from an eclectic array of nearly contemporary sources, not just spelunking for older examples of whatever it is you want to do. There's a degree to which this feels like splitting hairs to me – I mean, technically it's all past. Obviously we feel some palpable difference between something that came out last week or last year and something that came out in the 1970s (we're getting kind of close to the porous delineation between art and pop culture again), but reaching far or unexpectedly enough into the past can seem just as fresh as taking an idea from your contemporary – as we saw in the last chapter, plenty of avowedly avant-garde art plainly tried to source itself back to what it called primitive modes of art. Largely, though, I think we are just mistaking the distance of previous art for some kind of solidity, thinking that culture being born is somehow less pure than the stuff made by people who died long ago.

Consider, for instance, the television series *Stranger Things*. It is almost universally accepted to be a coming-of-age thriller wrapped around a nostalgia trip; the *Ready Player One*–esque yearning for the 1980s is assumed to be central to its appeal. Partly this is because of its setting, but mostly it's because the show also blatantly mimics the themes, styles, and even certain scenes of the pop culture of that era: its title lettering looks like it was torn off a Stephen King novel, its storylines track with films like *The Goonies, E.T., Firestarter, Red Dawn,* and *Invasion of the Body Snatchers,* and it even has actors of that era play off some of their notable roles, like *Aliens* corporate stooge Paul Reiser as a seemingly nefarious but unexpectedly helpful scientist. There are no doubt some nostalgic twinges in there, although much of this kind of discussion misses what is a reasonably original observation on the part of *Stranger Things*: namely that our view of an era like the eighties is so heavily mediated, so thoroughly dominated by its artifacts of pop culture, that one of the best ways to create a version of the era that feels accurate is to ape its style. In a sense, all these stylistic tics are just another form of set dressing that help immerse us in the story, help make it feel real and realized. The nostalgia in this case isn't incidental, but neither is it ill-considered: it's embraced and woven into the fabric of the art in a way that is reasonably unique and progressive.

Obviously, not all art is quite so clever or careful about what it's doing: some stuff is just dull revival or empty rehash, and nothing about collective taste or even critical appraisal is going to prevent sophisticated nostalgia from winning out over a simpler kind. But the point is more that our use of the word *nostalgia* is little more than a reaction to seeing something where the references are obvious to us, while the subtler necessity of reference in art escapes our notice.

The reason to be careful about this strange interplay goes beyond the fact that art tends to shape our understanding of nostalgia. Making art and indulging nostalgia are deeply sympathetic activities, fundamentally about giving meaning to the messy chaos of life. Art is not nostalgia exactly, but it is nostalgia-adjacent. While nostalgia comes about as a result of a haphazard, not entirely conscious, process, it is still fundamentally about recombining and reimagining our personal experiences to create some kind of meaningful whole, a sense of self. Art is more deliberate and particular, but it is also nothing more than a reordering of our experience into something comprehensible, unbound by the impossible necessity of being 'factual,' perhaps, but just as essential for helping us discover who and what we are. The underlying myth of nostalgia is that we make sense, that we can trace a path through our history into a comprehensive and coherent whole; the underlying myth of art is that any of this makes sense, that it means something at all. We desperately need both to keep going.

4

Great Again:
On Political Nostalgia

Nostalgia is not just an intensely personal experience, it is almost an exclusively personal one. This is true of essentially all our emotions: even when we are expressly sharing them with people, we are creating asymptotes, not braids, getting sympathetically close without ever losing the distinction of what is ours and what is theirs. Even if we are inspired into nostalgia by the same object, even if we are yearning for the same event or the same person, our experience of it will be, if not substantially different, at least meaningful in different ways, both occurring from different perspectives and spiralling out to suck in different references. If it's the notion of biting into a warm chocolate chip cookie that binds us, there is still something crucial to my experience that it is my grandmother's warm chocolate chip cookie, from her oven, in her kitchen, with the smell of impending prairie autumn coming through the windows and the chime of her old wooden clock ringing through the house, that gives the idea its tangible sense.

This sense is probably starker in nostalgia than in other emotions because nostalgia, as an aftershock of memory, the de facto substance of our self, is so helplessly tangled up with our identity: there is no meaningful way to separate who we are from what we are nostalgic about, much less how we are nostalgic. It's certainly true we can feel kinship or act as part of a group, but genuinely losing the boundary of ourselves and feeling a part of some greater whole generally requires drugs or some other religious ritual. And even in that case, there is always the comedown, and then we are alone again, with our own unique, untouchable nostalgia. (To my knowledge, no one has yet thought to ask people in the grips of a pan-conscious fervour whether they yearn for anything from their past, although anecdotally at least the people who are really into this kind of thing seem to think that desire of any kind is the realm of the hopelessly restricted individual, which I think proves my overall point here.)

This isn't to say that there aren't collective dimensions to nostalgia. Most of them, however – as we'll see in the next chapter – don't really try to fuse the personal aspects of nostalgic feeling, they just take advantage of the fact that there are sufficiently large lumps of close-enough touch points that it doesn't particularly matter if everyone is still clinging to their own experience. If you are programming a nineties dance night, for instance, the tent is big enough to accommodate the person who lost their virginity to 'More Than Words' playing in the tape deck of their '85 Chevette and the person who lost their virginity to 'More Than Words' playing in Winamp on their bedroom PC, to say nothing of the person whose graduation song was 'Good Riddance (Time of Your Life)' or the person who still has the costume they wore when they went as Britney Spears from the '… Baby One More Time' video. Honestly, even the concept of hiving off recent history into decades, as if the forces that acted on our lives carefully marked their calendars, is some indication of how collective nostalgia operates in a way that is fundamentally incoherent but practically functional: all it really needs to do is prompt a mass of individuals with some rough dates, and they will take care of the rest.

There is some element of this happening when nostalgia is evoked in the political realm. One of the foundational – if only fleetingly true – stories of modern democracy is that every individual matters a great deal; nostalgia is a powerful shortcut if you need to give a general appeal personal meaning, in the same way that the vagueness of horoscopes allows us to flood our circumstances into their predictions. A slogan like 'Make America Great Again' doesn't need to specify what or when constitutes 'great'; if it did, it would kneecap some of its inherent appeal. It doesn't say nothing, it says just enough to prompt someone to fill in the rest themselves. It's piping in the smell of warm cookies and letting you assume your grandma is in the kitchen.

Efficient messaging is only part of the political game, though, and in almost every other instance, nostalgic appeals in politics are more complicated, if not always more effective (although at the moment they do seem pretty goddamn effective). The art of politics in a democracy is getting people to subsume themselves into a mass movement. Any feeling that encourages people to meaningfully indulge their individuality is, if not entirely useless, at least a complicated dance: it means having to find resonant sympathies between an individual's identity and a movement's, having a person knowingly lower their boundaries of self but not lose them entirely. If you want to think in terms of political parties, it's the difference between appealing to your dyed-in-the-wool partisans and to the vaunted independents who swing elections. Numerous studies, in the U.S. and elsewhere, have suggested that the preferred party's position tends to dictate personal political views – in effect, most people in modern democracies have already outsourced their political identity entirely. Nostalgia's tendency to reinforce a sense of self can prove troublesome if it can't be efficiently married to a movement's sense of self.

The trickier issue with nostalgia in politics is that politics is explicitly about controlling the future. All nostalgia, of course, hums with this background dissonance – every aspect of life is about the future, whether we like it or not. But if nostalgia on a personal level acts as a balm or corrective, a way of futilely throwing ourselves at our past to help us get a firmer grasp on ourselves, nostalgia on the collective political level is not just impossible but meaningless besides. Our individual identity is troublesome enough, a shaky patchwork of self-aggrandizement and retroactive justification; the idea that there could be anything like an adequately encompassing identity for an entire populace that could be salvaged from the past collapses under its own absurdity. Even before we get into the longing, the suggestion of a monolithic identity that could be somehow unearthed would undercut the entire democratic project, since presumably any populace with that level of unity hardly needs to be asked about its preferences (this does at least roughly encapsulate nostalgia's appeal for fascists). Politicians who would have us believe that we must retreat to move forward are abdicating the responsibility of building a future for a chimera that's doubly impossible, delusion on top of confusion: not only is it impossible to go back, there is nothing of consequence to go back to anyway. To the extent that *nostalgia* is used as a slur in the political realm, this double helix of hopeless contradiction underlies it.

Not that contradiction has ever stopped anyone, least of all a political actor. In politics perhaps more than any other aspect of the world, intentionality can be a tricky thing to suss out. On the one hand, I'm not sure we can be too cynical about the political process or the motivations of people who are seeking political power, in whatever form or forum. If you were to go through life assuming that anyone trying to have some say in how things are to be run would do everything in their power to deceive you about the nature of themselves and their ultimate goals, you would probably end up a wise person. On the other hand, there is no deception more powerful than self-deception, and our fuzzy notions of authenticity virtually guarantee that the person most capable of feeding you a line of bullshit is the one who believes it wholeheartedly, even if they are merely the public facade of a vast, power-hungry machine. All of which is to say: though in general we will be discussing things as though they reflected a clear purpose, nostalgia is a messy tool, and one that people are not always aware they are wielding (even if only because it is important for their cause that they be ignorant of what exactly is in their hands).

In any event, in the case of political nostalgia – and maybe here we should be more precise and call it 'using or evoking nostalgia in the pursuit or consolidation of political power' – it's not simply a case of the blind convincing everyone else to shut their eyes. For all its contradictions, nostalgia also has some profound sympathies with political projects, sympathies that can and often do easily overwhelm rational chains of thought. Probably the most obvious is the fact that popular politics is usually trying very hard to overwhelm rationality, which makes a knee-jerk emotion like nostalgia incredibly useful. The emotions that tend to get the most play in politics are the kind that do not need to be nurtured or even, contra a popular reporter cliché, stoked, but that come without warning and must be forcibly pushed aside: anger or fear, for instance, work because they are merely reactions, involuntary responses that have to be dealt with even before we can decide if they're justified, let alone germane to the conversation we were trying to have.

Nostalgia is the same kind of rush, albeit often with a more positive, less aggressive halo: it comes without warning and leaves you distracted and lost, unable to identify, much less deal with, the issue at hand. It's an eternal reset button: in skilled hands it can reorient your priorities entirely; in lesser hands it is still a cheap enough trick that there's little to lose in trying it. And the only thing more foolish than falling for it again and again is assuming it never works.

As with nostalgic sloganeering, this short-circuit emotional aspect of nostalgia is usually left to the softer aspects of political power, the arts of persuasion and propaganda. But nostalgia also has powerful parallels in the more hard-headed application of political power, too. Because, although controlling the future is the end of politics, one of its means has always been to control the past, too. Exactly how depends on the situation: sometimes it can be a matter of making the current (and near-future) situation seem inevitable. We will talk more about this shortly, but we tend to see this in things like proto-nationalist movements, which often reorient the past into a long march of nationalist awakening. Often it is only something as nominally simple but morally complex as needing to erase an inconvenient or even diametrically opposed event from the cultural mythos, to preserve a story that casts ourselves as good and just: witness, because someone probably should, Canada's continuous refusal to reckon with the genocide, literal and cultural, of the Indigenous peoples who predate its formation, while styling itself as a global beacon of tolerance and understanding. Politics is power practically applied, and political histories will always attempt to make that power seem inevitable or righteous, if not both.

Whatever the exact reason, though, a political-minded history shares much with a nostalgic one: it is celebration through elision, a plucked-and-polished story that pretends it is encompassing; a memory that is prized for its utility, not its accuracy. The theorist and artist Svetlana Boym usefully separated nostalgia into two categories, reflecting the original portmanteau: restorative (*nostos*) and reflexive (*algia*). The latter is something like Fred Davis's second-order nostalgia, characterized by an interest in the longing for home and reflection of what home really means. (Which is to say: utterly useless and irrelevant in a political sense.) The former, though, captures the common root of both political history and political nostalgia: it is a restoration project, an attempt to rebuild what Boym calls the 'lost home,' and as such it is not only deeply unreflective but also often purposefully unaware of what it really is. As Boym puts it, restorative nostalgia 'does not think of itself as nostalgia, but as truth and tradition'; by the same token, political history does not regard itself as motivated, mutilated, or most convenient history. It is simply history, the way things were – or maybe, at worst, 'actually were,' if political power has recently changed hands and histories need a slight updating.

Not all political-historical projects will necessarily be nostalgic ones, of course: if anything, a good majority of political histories, particularly when we're talking about popular democratic politics, are very expressly trying to erase the past, not make you yearn to return to it. But when your base-level understanding of the past involves crafting a narrative in which you – however narrowly or broadly the lines of 'you' are drawn – are either history's most worthy successor or just a shining beacon in a fallen world, you will have a natural proclivity toward the nostalgic.

When a political force does get blatantly nostalgic – if only to its outside observers – it tends to benefit from a mutual reinforcement of simplicity. Mass features of nominally democratic politics naturally make it a game of diminished understanding; the cherished roles of propagandists, slogans, and empty figureheads reflect this as well as any modern op-ed columnist carrying on about the importance of 'messaging' and whether a politician is 'connecting with voters.' The goal is to find the simplest issue, the simplest idea, the simplest phrase that can turn people to your side. Nostalgia is simplicity through specificity. Even in a personal sense, though nostalgia can create complex emotional reactions or recollections, it is always inspired by very particular circumstances: we eat the cake and remember other cakes we've eaten, we feel lonely and think back to when we felt a part of something. It is a stimulus response, an effort to make some very particular ache fade away.

In a political sense, the easiest way to do this is to focus on a specific issue and then harken back to a time when that issue didn't seem to be a problem. Remember when there were jobs? Remember when your children could play outside by themselves? Remember when CEOs made only twenty times what workers made? Remember when you could afford a house? With the same set of biases that make us prone to nostalgia on a personal level – tending to both focus more on the good times and flatten them out into uncomplicated situations – this can be applied to nearly any specific complaint, regardless of the facts of the matter: as long as there is a perception that this particular issue was solved sometime before, turning toward the past provides an easy out.

In this light, the kind of complicating critiques that often follow nostalgic appeals are inevitably going to be ineffective. These typically take the form of granting the nostalgics that their perception about the past is right – it's hard to argue with a feeling, after all – but then suggesting that they are being too narrow-minded: say, for instance, that the 1950s might have indeed been better for the white middle class, but it came at the expense of almost everyone else. But, of course, the narrow-mindedness is the point: they're not holistically surveying society – if they were trying to make things better for everyone, they'd more likely be utopians than nostalgics – they are trying to solve a specific problem (it's harder out here for the white working class!). Granting them that their problem was solved but so many others weren't is like trying to convince a fish that most animals do just fine on land. You are better off trying to argue the feeling in the first place.

This intellectually convenient specificity works on another level, too, particularly as it pertains to anyone's most immediate concern: namely, how I, as an individual, am doing. This can seem to be a gloriously broad question, especially if you are accustomed to talking about politics on the socio-cultural level of most journalism and academics. When pollsters ask people where they think they are better or worse off, they also tend to include a whole host of other questions expressly attempting to drill down into more specificity: if things are worse, is it because there are more immigrants or fewer jobs, more inequality or less of a social safety net, too much crime or too many coddled youth? As useful as these are to understanding the broad outlines of societal forces, though, on the level of the individual they are bringing statistical analysis to a world with one data point. Survey after survey shows that the average voter, even on issues they regard as essential, is aware neither of on-the-ground realities nor of their own ignorance. Basic psychological studies suggest even the best informed of us are usually having gut-level reactions and concocting a complicated web of justifications for them. One of the simplest levels upon which a person can judge how things are going is 'Do I feel better today than I did yesterday (or last week, or six months or twelve years ago)?' If the answer is no, they will be susceptible to a nostalgic appeal of almost any stripe, and capable of conflating any number of big, complicated issues into one very specific and essential point.

Nostalgia's tendency to squash all issues into a political singularity is ultimately what lies at the core of its use in the political realm, or at the very least the political realm we've found ourselves in the for the last few hundred years. As I've alluded to a few times now, it is essentially a tool of identity, of helping you see yourself in whatever political project is trying to convince you to join it. And identity is at the core of the democratic project as we've defined it in the modern era: the imperative to have some say in how you are governed flows from your more basic right to decide who, or at least what, you are.

This is so utterly fundamental to how our politics operates that it can be easy to miss how non-essential to applications of political power it can be. In the monarchies and oligarchies that predate modern democracy, there were no campaigns of persuasion to convince your own populace of the rightness of policies, nor any attempt to win the hearts and minds of newly conquered peoples. How anyone without the ability to drum up an army felt about themselves was entirely irrelevant. Louis XIV did not refer back to the illustrious history of the Bourbon kings or even the glory of the French peoples to legitimate himself; when the state is moi, there is only one identity that matters. Certainly, the lack of meaningful mass identity was aided by a host of structural factors – poor literacy, subsistence living, really no information architecture to speak of – but it also did not begin factoring into the concerns of decision-makers until it led the people to start removing their decision-making heads. It's only once you've decided – or, really, been forced to accept – that people have some power that you need to start aligning with their self-conception.

How this works in practice, and the role of nostalgia in binding it together, is maybe easiest to understand by going back to the roots of sympathetic political identities, the nationalist projects that sprouted up across Europe during and after the eighteenth century. This is particularly true of the nationalistic sentiments of people who have tended to be occupied or otherwise oppressed by imperial forces. In the case of empires like the English, French, Russian, and Hapsburg, which ruled Spain and Austria, national identity tends to be formed more on the basis of conquest and potential: some reference to a glorious past is never out of place, but when you are in the process of subjugating foreign lands and peoples, you tend to build your identity more around your glorious present and glorious future (which, as ever, is assumed to be the present continuing on indefinitely). More Onward, Christian Soldier; less Remember Where You Came From.

France is an interesting study in this: its revolution, or at least the ideals that underlaid it, played a huge role in awakening nationalist fervour across the continent, and revolutionary imagery factors into many contemporary French symbols (if not always its actual day-to-day identity): the tricolour, Bastille Day, the national personification Marianne, etc. Nearly all of those symbols, however, were not adopted until almost a century after the revolution, in the time of the Third Republic. The interim was spent, of course, with Napoleon either conquering most of Europe or trying to work his way back from exile; it was only once France's prospects had diminished that its revolutionary near-past became an attractive national identity.

But the process is even clearer in nations that had to create an identity almost entirely whole-cloth. The first stage of most of these nationalist movements was getting people to recognize themselves as a group at all, a process that involved stitching together the customs and language of a specific geographic area into an identity that was somehow more meaningful than 'We all recognize these things.' In an essay on the necessity of creating a Polish government, Jean-Jacques

Rousseau identified this process as the most essential element, the act of infusing 'the soul of the parts throughout the whole of the nation; to establish the republic so strongly in the hearts of the Poles that she may survive in spite of all the efforts of her oppressors.'

From the vantage point of the modern era, where these identities are not so much something that needs to be cooked and swallowed as they are the lingering smell of the process, it can be hard to appreciate, but it takes a profound amount of work to turn, for instance, a person who happens to speak Polish or live in what people are now calling 'Poland' into a Polish person, whatever that really means. At its most basic level, and particularly at this time in history, you have to willingly forget that things like language and other bits of culture are the result of a range of individual or small-group sources slowly permeating up through a larger group. Instead you have to view this quality as an instantiation of some ethereal identity, some independent '-ness' given a beating heart solely by a collective belief in it.

And of course there is one other major complication. Like most revolutionary changes, whatever their populist pretensions, these movements were led by people who weren't so much powerless as simply not the most powerful – bourgeois merchants, second-rank nobles, the rich and educated tired of not being listened to. Even in barely literate, largely subsistence societies, it takes some doing to convince the peasants that their interests are tightly aligned with people who can all but buy and sell them. Whether this powerful underclass was restrained by their pretensions of humanistic self-determination or by the practicalities of not being able to bully people to go along with them is open to debate, but regardless, it left them in the same position: needing to persuade a mass of people that they had their interests at heart.

These factors – the necessity of a collective identity, the practical disparity of the movement's leaders from the people they purported to represent, and the general improbability of the latter forcefully overwhelming the former – helped contribute to a general sense among intellectuals of the time that a key factor for a worthwhile, let alone successful, nationalist movement was some kind of history of national identity. In his landmark 1861 work on self-determination, *Considerations on Representative Government*, John Stuart Mill said that the strongest case for a new national entity was a 'political antecedent.' This amounted to, in his formulation, '[t]he possession of a national history, and the consequent community of recollections; collective pride and humiliation, pleasure and regret, connected with the same incidents of the past.'

Mill was being descriptive as much as prescriptive: the underlying project of almost any nationalist movement – and, to a large degree, the determining factor in its support from nominal political allies and foreign intelligentsia – was to create the impression of not just a shared history but a specifically political sense of it. Unsurprisingly, a blinkered, overlrey simplistic, and pointedly rosy view of the past was practically a prerequisite. The result was the widespread use of, if not simple nostalgia per se, a kind of rampant meta-nostalgia, a yearning for people to have the yearning for a national past. These nationalist movements were effectively convincing people to be homesick for a house they were in the process of building.

One of the purest examples of how both this meta-nostalgia and, soon enough along, simpler nostalgia are used to form a mass identity can be found in Italy. Italy is at least a little unique insomuch as, of all the regions whose nationalist movements were fomented among generally oppressed peoples, it certainly has the most glorious actual history, if we're going to limit it to things that have happened within its current national boundaries. Exactly because of that, though, the process of creating a national identity is particularly tricky, and it's instructive to observe how Italy's history is used to solve contemporary problems but then reabsorbed or reinterpreted when different anxieties emerge. As with personal nostalgia, the political project of collective nostalgia is less about the past than about smoothing out the present by creating the impression of some coherent identity that has existed long before. (For whatever it's worth, recent polls have suggested that Italians are the most nostalgic nation in Europe, if not the world, which may have something to do with how steeped in nostalgia their formation was, but probably says more about how poorly they feel things are going – keeping in mind this research was done before the COVID-19 pandemic.)

Italian nationalism, which sprouted roots in the seventeenth and eighteenth centuries, then flowered into violence and ultimate unity in the nineteenth, was kind enough to plainly lay out its nostalgic delusions in its name: Il Risorgimento, The Resurgence. At the risk of offending Italian nationalists, who do not have a great history of self-effacement, there was hardly anything you could properly consider Italian to surge, much less re-. The thin, fancy boot that we now recognize had never previously considered itself a cohesive collective of the kind the nationalists were intent on creating. Depending on who exactly you asked, it had only ever even been unified, to the degree you can call it that, by imperialist foreign powers who were almost entirely heedless of the wishes and needs of the Italian people, which in these formulations usually meant anyone living on the peninsula who didn't have any power, although it could in a pinch be extended to the rich families who ruled cities but didn't enthusiastically collaborate with invaders (people like the Medici in Florence, or the Savoy in Sicily, who wound up being the kings of Italy until Italy stopped having such things).

Astute readers will have already begun wondering about Rome, the empire from which Western culture flows, but here is where we first start to run into the question of what political history, and yearning for a return to it, is really for. The glory of Rome was often explicitly evoked throughout the struggle to unify Italy – eventually. But, particularly in the early days of the Italian awakening, the past glory of Rome presented more of a problem for proper nationalists. Though it was hard to deny the geography, to say nothing of the linguistic and religious ancestry, Rome was a brutal, imperialist force – not just an Italian city that had started out conquering and subjugating its peninsular neighbours, but the model for most of Europe, including the dynasties that were currently occupying most of contemporary Italy. One early nationalist leader went so far as to say that, given the option, he would 'tear the pages of Roman history to shreds,' as they were 'written with the blood of peoples, [the] enslavement of nations.' For the purpose of trying to forge a nation from under the yoke of imperial rule, Rome was a glorious past but a horrible metaphor.

The unfortunate optics of Italy's most obvious political progenitor did not make the need for one any less pressing, however. This led Italian nationalists, particularly in their more nascent, philosophical stages, down some bizarre rabbit holes. Some of these involved garden-variety nationalist nostalgia, like reimagining notable medieval and Renaissance Italian-speakers as explicit precursors to an expressly Italian state. Dante was not just a philosophical poet: he prefigured the glories of the Italian people by writing in their own language. (By his own admission, he was just trying to give the common people 'crumbs of bread from the table of wisdom' – which is to say clerical Latin, which even he admitted was more beautiful and suited to the study of knowledge than the vulgar tongues.) Machiavelli became not just a sharp-tongued, satiric republican, poking holes in the logic of local principalities, but a voice rallying for the freedom of Italian people, pluralistically.

By far the oddest trend in Italian national nostalgia, though, was the eighteenth-century fever for Etruscheria, a sort of Beatlemania for bullshit anthropology. This obsession centred on the Etruscans, a jumped-up city state that, both prior to and since the early stages of Italian nationalism, has been understood to be a minor-key prelude to the Roman symphony. For a few hundred years, from about 750 BCE to 500 BCE, they were the major player in the area around modern Tuscany and Lazio; like most city states of the peninsula, they were heavily influenced by the Greeks and were eventually swallowed up by the Romans. Their resurgence began in earnest in the eighteenth century, when nationalists desperate for a model they could follow began to ascribe to them near-mythic importance. That is not an exaggeration: at least one respected scholar argued that the advanced Etruscan society was the basis for the myth of Atlantis. Only slightly more realistically, the Etruscans were said to be the real source of not only Roman but also Greek culture. Their empire, it was theorized, rather conveniently stretched across the Italian peninsula, with nearly identical borders to modern-day Italy, and had been occupying this area since before recorded history.

These stories of unprecedented, explicitly Italian glory lingered until less explicitly nationalistic scholars had a chance to sift through the Etruscan rubble in the late eighteenth and early nineteenth centuries. Just in the nick of time, the understanding of Rome was rehabilitated, and it took its place as the obvious political precedent among the mélange of misappropriated medieval city states and jury-rigged Italian-speakers. By the time the nationalist rebels briefly occupied Rome in 1849, the name of both the government they founded and the leaders who administered it – the Roman Republic and the triumvirate – were expressly meant to evoke what they conceived of as the peak of the ancient era. Nothing about the papal or Hapsburgian competition for the soul of Italy, nor Roman history, had actually changed, of course: the only real difference was the nationalists' lack of other plausible antecedents. And without some sense of history, this nationalist project would seem like nothing more than a power grab by a small group of rich men and nobles more upset by who sat at the top of the pyramid than by the shape of the country itself. Considering that the result of all this nationalist fervour and war was a new king, a renewed commitment to the church, and a languishing liberal-democratic project whose failures directly contributed to the creation of Fascism as an ideology, it was a good thing for their own self-interest that the nationalists had something else to hang their hook on.

The shape of Italian political nostalgia from then on will look more familiar to us. Mussolini's Fascism was deeply nostalgic, and began with reinterpreting the Risorgimento, bleeding it of the democratic ideals that – all cynicism about certain of its leaders aside – were heavily represented in both its inspiration and many of its fiercest fights. In Mussolini's recasting, it instead became an example of will to power, a raw land grab that inspired Mussolini's often shifting ideology and his endeavours in Africa and the Second World War. He saved his deepest yearnings for the Romans, however. He frequently harkened back to them in speeches – 'My journey means the strengthening of the Italian power which has descended from Ancient Rome,' he once told a group in Sicily, an area not renowned for its love of Roman people of any era. He adopted imperial imagery like the eagle, made a holiday of Rome's founding, built neoclassical monuments to invoke Rome's imperial glory, and even took the name of his movement from the fasces, the ancient Roman symbol of magisterial power.

Mussolini has by now become a source of nostalgia in his own right, although it is of generally the same flavour as his own: a kind of nationalistic consolidation, emphasizing choice aspects of a history to create a focused conception of a country's identity. This is undoubtedly the form of political nostalgia most familiar to us now, likely because, though national identity is as fungible and intangible as any other identity, it is the one our political organization principle of nation-states attaches the most meaning to, suggesting a palpable quality that isn't entirely there but must always be reached for. (Given that most political power doesn't cross borders, it also probably doesn't hurt that political actors can be relatively sure that their entire audience probably identifies at least a little with any national identity they're trying to promote: UN officials don't often wax poetic about the glories of whatever country they're from.)

But the precise identity is not really the point: the point is that, for any modern political project, a certain sense of identification is necessary. In the same way that Poles and Italians first had to be convinced that they were Poles and Italians, modern democratic citizens first need to be convinced that any issue they're going to support aligns with their self-conception – that they are *the kind of people* who would support raising marginal tax rates or banning abortion or building bike lanes or removing development restrictions. And though it is not the only way, one of the most direct and potent ways of doing that is to suggest to them that they were already that kind of person, and could be again – that all they have to do is go back to the way they were, that we have to go back to the way we were.

This sort of appeal tends to be associated, in contemporary politics, with conservatives, and in fairness, a movement that is explicit about preserving and maintaining the mores of society is going to have more occasion to yearn for the way things used to be. But it is by no means an exclusively conservative tendency: if the stereotypical North American conservative seems to yearn for the suburbification and nominal unity of the 1950s, the stereotypical progressive is often just as open about pining for the direct political action and mass movements of the 1960s. There is even a vogue among more explicit leftists to harken back to the days of the high marginal tax rates and resolute middle class of the postwar era. The only real prerequisite for a nostalgic appeal is an issue that requires identification – which is to say, any of them – and a reasonably plausible story that things once were better than they are currently. Armed with these, there is no end to the permutations of nostalgia, offering people a plausible explanation of who they are and why the kind of person they are should vote for whatever it is I am saying they should vote for.

This broadness is certainly part of what makes nostalgia so easy to dismiss in the political realm: it is so frequently used, and so easy to deploy, that it hardly seems to mean much of anything, and as such is easy to spot and even easier to denigrate. We should be careful with throwing around *nostalgia* as an easy insult, though, something to dismiss out of hand. The simplest reason is that we will only ever levy the charge against something we disagree with anyway: wrong-headed ideas about the past are nostalgia, but the ones we agree with are the truth. Carelessness on this front seems like an easy way to get yourself sucked into a blatantly nostalgic appeal.

It is also a good way to miss some very real problems in the world. Chalking something up to mere nostalgia overlooks the possibility that things are indeed worse for the people indulging in it, that they have every reason to look back with envy. How much that could or should be mitigated, of course, depends on a great many factors, but there is a substantial difference, particularly in the political realm, between choosing how to address an issue and being entirely unaware or unconcerned with it. The Venn diagram of people who laughed heartily at Make America Great Again hats and people who were completely bowled over by Donald Trump becoming president is close to a perfect circle; casual dismissal does nothing to diminish a frothing undercurrent.

Also, not that this is a problem with nostalgia so much as our reaction to it, but it would pay to be vigilant to what you are willing to dismiss as 'nostalgia,' because that can be a very nice way of putting something down. Nostalgia has two vectors, after all: what is being yearned for and the yearning itself. People who dismiss others' nostalgia are often denigrating the impossible lust to return without really thinking about what the longing is for; the fact that you even recognize a nostalgic longing in someone else does inherently suggest you have some sympathy or understanding for what it is they are longing for, and it would pay to make yourself aware of why that might be. Without litigating this too hard, it does not seem to be for nothing that white supremacists and other racists are given the benefit of being dismissed as nostalgic, whereas the conservative elements of other cultures – a woman wearing a hijab, say – are not afforded the same sympathy.

Because, for all the potential broadness of political nostalgia, the most notable thing about its effects is how seriously it constricts the world. In other instances of collective nostalgia, the grouping together of multiple nostalgias – still retaining their basic experiential independence – tends to enhance and enrich our nostalgic feeling. At the very least, no one nostalgia erases any other; we may be alone in our specific feeling, but we are alone together. The nature of political identity, the necessity of group solidarity, the kind of story that political movements must fabricate, creates an inevitably exclusive nostalgia. Political nostalgia is a nostalgia that cannot allow any other nostalgias to exist, because to do so would mean weakening the identity that is trying to be built. How can you be meaningfully Italian if you are also strongly Sicilian? How can you be truly committed to building affordable housing if you're sitting in your kitchen wringing your hands about property values? People in their private multitudes can reconcile these things quite easily; political identities are too fragile to allow such a multiplicity of views, because they put the lie to the story. The comforting surety of identity is one of the intoxicating appeals of political projects.

This is what is often terrifying about political applications of nostalgia: the erasure contained within them. It is not just that by praising the fifties as a golden era of white middle-class achievement you are erasing the current concerns of people who disagree with you – it is that you are erasing their history, too. Historian Tony Judt touched on this problem when diagnosing the troubles in Eastern Europe in the wake of the collapse of the Soviet Union: they had 'too much memory, too many pasts on which to draw, usually as a weapon against the past of someone else.' Pasts are no less a source of conflict than present issues; as a kind of colonization of the past, an insistence that it fit a shape that addresses very specific, modern needs, politically influenced nostalgia flattens all other pasts, making them not just impermissible but illegible, nonsensical responses to the political issues of the day, identities that cannot be identified.

Ultimately, political nostalgia is about yearning to return not to any real collective past but to one winnowed down to some essential truth. Nostalgia threatens us most the instant it is sure it's not nostalgia at all, but truth.

5

A Breath of Relief from This Fast-Paced World: On Consumed Nostalgia

Among the most consistent and popular posts on the nostalgia subreddit, one of the internet's foremost collective repositories of recollection and reminiscence, are images of toys. Most of these toys tend to be derived from the childhood sweet spot of the first few generations with mass computer literacy, which is to say the mid-to-late eighties, nineties, and, more frequently now, the early 2000s. There is a mild tendency toward slightly more techy toys like video game systems – which are more than mere toys now but certainly weren't in the time most people are recollecting – but, Reddit reflecting the relentless interest of the crowd, no other real organizing principle beyond a rough timeline: Etch A Sketches and Easy-Bake Ovens show up as often as action figures and Pogs.

Toys are a natural focus for nostalgic inspiration: they are so ubiquitous throughout childhood that the act of putting them away for good is synonymous with growing up, giving them a symbolic weight that might well be unmatched, except maybe among certain childish foods. As objects, they are a natural repository for memory, and since presumably most of those memories are both positive and social – playing with siblings and friends, getting a special present from a relative, bragging to a classmate about that exact same present – they are ideal stuff for frequent, fond recollection. If play is truly as important as the psychologists think for forming full-blown humans from the primordial soup of childhood, toys might even represent some crucial aspect of our personality, stand-ins for formative experience or essential aspect of who we are.

The toys of this particular cohort of people, though, are unique from the dolls and board-game pieces that have counted as childhood amusements for at least as long as there has been society. Part of it is the simple fact that we live in an age of mass production, where it is easy for us to produce exact replicas of the things we might be yearning for: my grandmother might never have found an exact replica of the cloth doll her grandmother made for her, whereas I can go out and buy Barbies cut from the very same moulds – or at least the same patterns of moulds – that my mother would have had. More potent than the toys' substance, though, is their psychological setting: thanks to a sustained rise in influence of market-based decisions on what constitutes appropriate mass communication toward children, and concurrent deregulation of advertising standards and television programming, any child born after roughly the mid-seventies – at least in advanced Western economies, and maybe most particularly in North America – has been subject to a ubiquitous and relentless marketing effort meant to ensure that those toys would become an essential and meaningful part of their childhood (at least until next season's batch came along). Barring the most steadfast wood-working grandparent or paranoid unplugged parent, it is virtually guaranteed that at least one of the most beloved childhood nostalgia objects – if not the vast majority – of everyone from Gen X forward will be the end result of millions of dollars, hundreds of creative minds, and dozens of carefully placed and nurtured messages designed to create exactly that situation. These nostalgic recollections on an internet message board are as much a function of personal passion as they are an aftershock of capitalism starting the engine on its next generation of consumers.

In the case of our reminiscing redditors, at least, the nostalgia is only a by-product of the more general marketing force, a side effect of having successfully convinced someone to buy the right thing in a moment particularly susceptible to forming important memories. In our modern age of almost unfettered consumption, though, most of the intersection of nostalgia and something worth buying is considerably more deliberate, carefully triggered, enhanced, and exploited at nearly every available opportunity. Being prodded into consumption might well be the most consistent source of nostalgic feelings we have, and though neither side of that equation may, strictly speaking, need the other, they do share a natural affinity that often enhances or deepens our experience of both. They are so compatible that there is almost certainly a direct link between our growing awareness of nostalgia as a phenomenon over the last century and its effectiveness as a marketing tactic in a world increasingly at the mercy of a system that demands unlimited consumption. (It is even possible, though a harder case to make, that some of the enthusiasm we have shown for consumerism is due to its ability to seemingly solve our nostalgic yearnings, although I'll come back to that.)

This isn't to suggest that nostalgic longing was in any way created by a consumerist society to help move more product. But if that longing had not already existed, it might have been necessary to create it: nostalgia – the way it makes us feel, the things it inspires us to do, its function in our personal sense of meaning and identity – is an almost perfect impulse for a consumerist ethic, an essential facet of our being that is utterly symbiotic with the drives and desires necessary for a consumptive society to function smoothly.

The root of this affinity is in the insatiable, gnawing longing inherent to both nostalgia and consumerism. Both are about consistently indulging impossible desires, playing out patterns that are as hopeless to escape as they are to resolve. If this fundamental contradiction is not exactly the highest purpose of both, it is their animating influence, the thing that ultimately gives them meaning. In this ceaseless tension, nostalgia and consumerism suggest something to us about our ultimate purpose, or at least purport to give us some greater clarity about who we are, and better equip us to find out what that might be. The notable difference in them is that, for nostalgia, the fleeting nature of this clarity is its deepest tragedy; for consumerism, it's the highest triumph. Still, this ultimate antipathy in their meaning and how people use them hasn't kept the two concepts from being intimately connected from even the earliest days of consumer culture.

Consumerism shares another similarity with nostalgia: its sheer ubiquity can make it a difficult concept to pin down. The modern vogue for the word apparently owes its roots to a 1955 speech by John Bugas, who was then the second-in-command of the Ford Motor Company. He suggested it explicitly as a substitute for *capitalism*: 'The term "consumerism" would pin the tag where it actually belongs – on Mr. Consumer, the real boss and beneficiary of the American system.' Appropriately enough, considering how dependent a consumerist ethic is on marketing and branding, this was less about clarity and more a case of trying to make something – namely barely restrained capitalism – more palatable (or at least harder to fight). 'It would pull the rug right out from under our unfriendly critics who have blasted away so long and loud at capitalism,' Bugas went on. 'Somehow, I just can't picture them shouting: "Down with the consumers!"' Though Bugas's haloed version of the word persists, particularly as a supposedly value-neutral economic term, it took half a decade for the word to acquire a more negative connotation. In his 1960 book, *The Waste Makers*, Vance Packard, a mid-century critic of marketing and corporate-influenced society in general, portrayed consumerism as a core feature of America's moral rot, representing materialism and harmful excess – a critical conception that has stuck around ever since, and is arguably the more common connotation.

Whatever inherent value you attach to the term, Bugas is right insomuch as consumerism can be understood to be the practical application of capitalism – one of the engines that allows the theory to work, maybe its most persistent and ubiquitous function, and the way in which it actually plays out in our day-to-day lives. Essentially, it is the idea that the most important economic role a person has is as someone who buys things, to the point where simply consuming is an end in itself, prone to delivering a host of effects that are crucial for a prosperous, smoothly functioning society – the main one being that it keeps money flowing.

That money even has any purpose but to flow from one person to the next is a concept that is not so much foreign to us as utterly alien. (As modern philosopher Omar Little so eloquently put it, 'Money ain't got no owners, only spenders.') We are very much encouraged to believe – and judging by rates of consumer debt, boy do we – that any and all money beyond what's required for our basic upkeep exists solely to satisfy some previously unattainable, if not undreamt of, desire. If you are among the world's wealthiest and most powerful, this has more or less always been the case. For everyone else, this attitude is very much a modern invention: as Colin Campbell explains in his history of consumer culture, *The Romantic Ethic and the Spirit of Modern Consumerism*, until roughly eighteenth-century London, if you were able to secure any excess wealth, odds were it went to either saving for inevitable lean times or paying someone else to do your work for you. The notion that the average person might use wealth simply to steadily acquire more things was so anti-thetical, it was an issue of severe, and settled, morality. We can get a taste of this in the reaction to Bernard Mandeville's 1714 book, *The Fable of the Bees*, a poem-and-essay combination that advocated for loose spending and indulgence in personal luxuries as a tool for a more prosperous society. It was heartily denounced: Mandeville was convicted of being a public nuisance, his book decried as a monstrous affront to good Christian virtues. This was probably one of his main goals. In any case, he was acutely aware that he was prodding prevailing morality – the book's subtitle was *Private Vices, Publick Benefits*. Beyond the moral outrage, though, that

Mandeville even needed to argue that profligate consumption was necessary and good may be enough of a sign of how different times were.

Even in outraged England, meaningful mass opposition to the idea of consumption for its own sake almost entirely dissipated in less than eighty years. Certainly by the turn of the century, London and its environs in particular were an almost rampant consumer society: one contemporary observer noted that not only the type but the sheer number of things the typical middle-class family had in its home – everything from sugar, the consumption of which increased twentyfold in England over the course of the eighteenth century, to glassware and useless *objets d'art* – would have baffled their ancestors from even a few generations before. Fashions began to change so rapidly that it was said you could tell how far you were from London based on how old the patterns used for making clothes were. And this consumption was no longer a matter of wealth: though fine furniture and fancy jewellery might be limited to the aristocratic classes and their nearest adjacents, even poorer people started buying ready-made meals at inns and taverns or shopping for fresh produce at newly established markets. Everyone had found something to spend money on; our world had taken shape.

If it is plainly obvious that the world changed, though, why it changed is trickier to answer, but also revealing of why nostalgia and consumerism are such harmonious forces. The high school textbook explanation is that the combination of the plunder of colonial empire and the production power of the Industrial Revolution was capable of creating both a lot more stuff for people to buy and a lot more wealth to buy it with. This is more of a material cause than a reason for a change in outlook, though: as a foodie at a buffet will tell you, something's ready availablity does not mean it will necessarily be desired – the desire to consume needs to be created.

From our current vantage point, we might just think of that desire as something like hunger: a natural inclination toward consumption beyond our necessities. There's perhaps something to this: humanity's track record of extincting megafauna certainly suggests that we may not have a solid concept of what exactly constitutes our basic needs – and again, very few wealthy people in the history of society have ever found any reason to not lavish themselves with whatever luxuries they could find or create. On the other hand, the entire history of arts and recreation would suggest that humanity has plenty of other things to do with our time once we're warm and full, even if these aren't entirely separable from the drive to consume. At the very least, if consumption at modern levels is some latent innate drive, it's one that requires not just inspiration but consistent nudging to be acted on.

Fortunately for the forces of consumption, there is a more definitive innate drive that works as one hell of a nudge: social pressure. There is almost nothing that means quite as much to people as their admission and standing within a preferred group, and whether it's the subtle nastiness of peer pressure or the lofty ideals of humanist utopia, being accepted is a root cause for almost everything humans regard as good, rationally and irrationally. According to this line of thought, the sudden mass production of luxuries finally allowed people other than the ludicrously wealthy to fill their less material needs; among the biggest of those is trying to fit in among the ludicrously wealthy or, anyway, to project social status through nice stuff.

This is the theory Thorstein Veblen advances in his landmark 1899 work, *The Theory of the Leisure Class*, which gave us the concept of conspicuous consumption: consumer culture is fuelled by our need to project what kind of people we are, especially to the kind of people we want to be. Veblen observed that one of the essential drivers of purchasing patterns – usually most identifiable in fads – was social emulation: what late twentieth centuryists called keeping up with the Joneses, but what to eighteenth- and nineteenth-century Britons would have been as simple as imitating the aristocracy, and then imitating the merchant class who were imitating the aristocracy, and then imitating the middle class who were imitating the merchants, and so on down the line.

Veblen's explanation is buoyed by the fact that some of the earliest creators of consumer goods exploited this tendency to make themselves rich and powerful. Josiah Wedgwood was one of England's greatest potters, creating a company whose tableware is esteemed for its craftsmanship to this day. He is also more or less the creator of modern advertising: he did not invent the concept of fine china, but he is almost certainly the reason every home has a set of it collecting dust somewhere. Wedgwood had an almost dizzying array of techniques to convince people to buy his stuff – he is credited with inventing, among other things, direct mail and illustrated catalogues, travelling salesmen, and even buy-one-get-one-free promotions – but his greatest trick was getting it in the hands of nobles and aristocracy and then making sure everyone else knew they had it. He would name entire lines of pottery after the notables he created the originals for – Queen's Ware (Queen Charlotte),

Royal Pattern (duh), Russian Pattern (Catherine the Great) – and even took to displaying custom pieces he made for those royals and aristocrats in his boutiques for months before delivering them. This tactic has proved so successful you can now make a pretty decent living just by posting pictures and videos of yourself using products, so long as you and your life are sufficiently attractive to the right demographic.

Still, if openly displaying how much you fit in is central to consumer culture, that likely says more about how important social bonds are than it explains the roots of consumerism. In the same way that nostalgia's preoccupation with social connections is a function of how important social cohesion is to who we are, it seems more likely that social posturing is an inextricable part of consumerism because it's an inextricable part of everything we do. From ceremonial dress to religious iconography, humans broadcast what groups we belong to, and it is only natural that that tendency would shape a widespread phenomenon. That there are profound sympathies between finding ways to fit in and buying things that help you fit in might explain why consumerism has become a dominant, society-spanning force, but even mutually assured benefits still don't explain why the relationship should have ever started.

Within the notion of conspicuous consumption, though, is the idea that underlies the real crux of consumer society, the one that makes nostalgia such a natural impulse. In trying to signal our group affiliation, we are inherently trying to tell people who we are – specifically, that we are people like them. But even that recognition requires us to make some kind of sense of ourselves: we have to recognize not just that we are individuals but that that individuality means something, that it is crucial for us to understand and act on our individual desires.

That we should have any other kind of understanding is again a counterintuitive idea from where we sit: even if much of it is ultimately lip service, the reigning importance of individual drives is inextricable from our world, from the notion of human rights through democracy on up. And, in fairness, it is not so much that we as individuals recognize our importance that's actually important here – individually, we put that together fairly quickly after our consciousness flickers on. It's that society as a whole regards our individuality as meaningful, as something to be not only considered but promoted. As Campbell explores in *The Romantic Ethic*, for England in the eighteenth century, this idea would have flickered through early Christian thought, started getting some real promotion during the Renaissance, and gradually become the bedrock truth upon which society was based via the Enlightenment. It was the intellectual ether for revolutions around Europe, the spark of the Romantic movement in arts that is arguably still our dominant mode of creating and understanding things – Campbell convincingly argues that Romantic novels were among the most important spurs for further consumption, devoted as they were to encouraging readers to let the heart want what it wants – and it reached popular prominence just as companies had the ability to make and the need to sell a cornucopia of dubiously necessary stuff. Stuff that, with this new understanding of the individual, could not just occupy roughly the same space as you but help define you.

If this is the spark of consumerism, though, it is not actually the motor. Other attempts to reconcile the importance of the individual in society have, if not actual endpoints, at least higher expressions that both absorb and buttress this individual instinct. In the political realm, democracy becomes the ultimate expression of the individual, and so the individual ethos can be poured into expanding and protecting it for its own ends. Art becomes an opportunity to understand yourself, a project that constantly moulds itself to fit the new contours of a life. Consumerism cannot offer a meaningful end point to the individual: it can offer definition, but it can never be definitive. Its highest purpose is not to help us understand who we are, it's to keep the economy moving. There must always be demand for something else: its answers have to be fleeting, its definitions constantly changing; it is built to use itself up and offer fresh new meanings with every season. This instability is fundamental: after all, if enough middle-class merchants buy enough aristocratic dinnerware, it's hardly a mark of the aristocracy anymore. Consumerism runs on an individualism of gnawing desire, of want so profound it feels like need, even if it's ultimately insatiable.

This is the mechanism of nostalgia: a yearning that's impossible to deny and impossible to destroy. To experience a desire that can never be truly fulfilled is the process of a nostalgic and the purpose of a consumer. This fearful symmetry is what makes nostalgia such a useful force for consumerism. Unlike many other moods and feelings, tapping into nostalgia doesn't require creating a desire, only promising to fill the lack that already exists. It doesn't matter that the promise is hollow, or at least temporary: fleeting satisfaction, bittersweetness, and a perpetual sense of incompleteness are inherent, even crucial, to the full experience. Consumerism seeks to turn every desire into something like nostalgia, something momentarily overwhelming, temporarily tamed, and always ready to be triggered again. They are mutually reinforcing, a double helix of irresolvable mood: nostalgia primes us for consumerist want, and the perpetual background hum of this desire makes the frustrated yearnings of nostalgia feel all the more comfortable and correct.

But it's not just the mechanisms that support each other. Though its essential yearning is irreconcilable, nostalgia, like consumerism, does offer some relief in the form of definition. As we have seen, though we cannot return to whatever moment we're pining for, we can learn something about who and what we are simply by understanding what it is we want to return to. Nostalgia is one of our most potent methods of creating the self, something like the greatest-hits collection of what we want to be, who we think we are. In this, consumerism's aims are the same, albeit usually wrapped in the promise that becoming something different is merely the right purchase away. Again, though, what you might become, or what you might have been, are secondary concerns: within both consumerism and nostalgia, you are what you desire, and this fleeting definition is as much resolution as either can – or wants to – offer.

So it is only natural that, even before nostalgia was understood as a basic fact of the human experience, it was being employed by the forces of consumerism to help move units. Unsurprisingly, it reveals itself most frequently in advertising – consumerism's language, its method for instilling desire – but it can occasionally burrow itself into the very fabric of products, too. Among Wedgwood's biggest sellers, for instance, were neoclassical vases that he labelled 'Etruscan,' after the faddish interest of the time. Done in the style of

Greek (because they didn't know any better) and, yes, Etruscan pottery that had been recently unearthed in Italy, these vases presented classical-like scenes that had been toned down and cleaned up for contemporary English sensibilities – covering up the offensive bits of the past so that they could be more easily and widely sold. Wedgwood was selling a rosy recreation of the past – and his taste for it went far beyond a mere style. He built an entire factory, which he named the Etruria Works, exclusively for the creation of this line. Its motto was, of course, Latin: *Artes Etruriae Renascuntur*: 'The arts of Etruria are reborn.' He owned enough land around the factory that he was able to rename the entire district Etruria – a name that persists to this day – and even built a large house, Etruria Hall, across the river from the factory. The house was important enough to him that he lived out his final days there. Nostalgia moved beyond a mere marketing technique to become a serious part of Wedgwood's own self-identification – although, in fairness to him, his own works would seem to be the only rival to the ancient artifacts that inspired them, and these days his originals are almost as prized, in certain circles.

Nostalgic inflections shaded plenty of products and pitches for them throughout the nineteenth century, but as with most things related to consumer society, things really exploded in America in the middle of the twentieth century. Marketing strategy, in particular, owes most of its sophistication to the rise of the Depth Boys, researchers influenced by the burgeoning fields of psychology and psychoanalysis, who started to form the strategic spines of marketing firms in the 1930s, '40s, and '50s. Picking up on the insights of public relations guru Edward Bernays – who himself was translating the insights of his uncle Sigmund Freud to the realm of mass communication – marketers began to codify and systematize how they were appealing to consumers, by exploring the unconscious drives and internal psychological needs they could potentially fulfill.

Our old consumerism critic Vance Packard was one of the first to explore the rise of these tactics in his 1957 book, *The Hidden Persuaders*. Through interviews with contemporary marketers and researchers, he laid out a handful of underlying drives – things like emotional security, ego gratification, a sense of roots – that campaigns attempted to tap into. The underlying logic, though, was summed up by one consultant who was helping to brand gasoline: 'In buying gasoline you get played back to who you are. Each gasoline has built up an image or a personality. Each helps a buyer answer the question "Who am I?"' This is the consumerist promise of self-invention spelled out. And though the function of marketing since its invention has been to marry the individual's idea of who they are and what they want with the notion that a product or service will help them fulfill that, marketers now began crafting their pitches explicitly with that goal in mind – and realized quite quickly that tapping into their past, especially if it was sanitized and shined, was a shortcut to meaning that tended to cut across multiple underlying drives.

Though the concept of nostalgia was still a little too nebulous to be employed by name, the concentrated effort to craft advertising that resonated not just emotionally but with a particular self-image effectively created the first ads where attempting to trigger nostalgic longing was the express purpose, not just happenstance or intuition. Packard shows how this process worked for a counterintuitive product:

freezers. If not exactly space-age technology, in the 1940s they were on the cutting edge of kitchen appliances, one of a host of new gadgets that were supposed to make modern life easier and more convenient. Their primary problem at the time was that they were hardly economical: between the electricity costs of keeping them running and the fact that people had a tendency to forget they had stored food in them and end up throwing a significant portion of it away, freezers actually tended to increase overall kitchen costs. By interviewing people who bought them, researchers discovered freezers were associated not with efficiency or convenience but with security. Thinking about all the food in the freezer reminded owners of the last time they were safe and secure and never had to worry about where food was coming from – which for most people was when they were children. So, ads that had previously touted technical specs and modernity instead began throwing the consumer back into the world of the child: doting moms stood in front of stocked freezers, children's characters like Alice explored the wonderland of frozen food, a child nearly fell into a Frigidaire freezer while being asked to 'pick a pack of frozen peppers.' Modern convenience became a return to the safety and security of childhood, while freezers became a standard part of every refrigerator and kitchen.

The kind of psychological deep-dive research that came into vogue around this time – or perhaps, more accurately, the interpretative leaps made from this kind of market research – can be of dubious value: like a lot of psychoanalysis, it tends to say more about the psyche of the person interpreting the findings than about the subjects, and subsequent research suggests that the feelings underlying whether or not we buy something tend to be more like fleeting moods than primal urges. Nevertheless, creating a deep, basic identification with a product – or now, more typically, an entire brand – is still central to the practice of marketing, and nostalgia has been one of its most effective tools, rising in prominence in society in general as it became a staple of branding efforts.

Nostalgia has enough profile in the consumerist world that the spiritual descendants of those original Depth Boys have subjected it to prolonged study, with a minimum of psychoanalysis mixed in. Business and marketing researchers were among the first to pursue substantive psychological assessments of how nostalgia works, albeit almost entirely limited to how it affects whether or not you're willing to buy things. They have so far largely found a mixed bag. In the eighties and nineties, Morris Holbrook determined that nostalgia proneness was an identifiable characteristic of people, a personality trait that transcended age, gender, and, for the most part, the era evoked; he also proposed an index you could use to figure out where your target audience landed on the scale, and noted that the period of their lives for which people tended to feel the strongest nostalgia was from age fourteen to twenty-four. Several studies co-authored by Darrel D. Muehling suggest that using nostalgia is far more likely to elicit a strong emotional response, positive or negative. Conventional advertising wisdom is that people buy with their feelings, not their heads, and the viewer's emotional response overshadows the actual messaging of an ad. One of the more curious studies comes from, among others, Kathleen Vohs, Land O'Lakes chair in marketing at the University of Minnesota: it suggests that nostalgia's established tendency to make people feel more socially connected also has the effect of making them care less about money, and thus makes them more prone to buy whatever is being advertised. (Though the relatively short-term emotional effects suggest that the forces of consumerism might be better off priming people for nostalgia in situations where they're able to buy something in short order, like an online or IRL store.)

One thing nearly all the studies agree on, though, is that nostalgia, appropriately, tends to make the ad at least more memorable, and that in and of itself may be enough reason to explain its ongoing prevalence in marketing. It's hardly appropriate for all contexts, but still, there is almost no category of product or service that can't be loaded with nostalgia, as long as the nostalgia-prone are at least part of the audience you're targeting. Food, tied up as it is in formative experiences with friends and family, seems to be the most natural category, but cars, furniture, clothing, video games, movies, music – a dizzying amount of modern entertainment, really – and basically everything else with more than about a decade of history can and almost certainly has been the subject of at least one prominent campaign whose underlying pull was nostalgia. Whatever it's selling, though, nostalgic marketing tends to fall into one of two categories, with overlapping tactics but distinct goals. Marketing researcher Barbara B. Stern defines these as 'historical' and 'personal' nostalgias: either the brand or product attempts to imbue itself with a nostalgic import (historical) or it tries to invoke the consumer's private nostalgic feelings and graft them onto whatever is being sold (personal).

Of the two, historical nostalgia tends to be the more obvious, and the type more frequently indulged. It was what Wedgwood was after with his faux-Etruscan pottery, and is probably most noticeable these days in the searchingly trendy independent products that fight off their inherent modernity by making their logos look like they were torn off dry goods from a frontier general store: the single-source chocolate bars, apothecary-inflected cosmetics, and small-batch gin bottles primarily marketed to downtown millennials. All these products represent the ends of what is an unbroken chain. Though some, including Stern, think that nostalgic ads are especially prominent in times of societal upheaval (like the 1960s) or prominent moments in the passage of time (like the turn of the millennium), there have been products in any era that market themselves as allowing you to return to some earlier, better era, whether that's antiquity or just the first-wave punk scene.

These sorts of advertising tactics tend toward roughly the same promise that Stern found in the 1980s direct-order catalogue *Victoria*, which sold exclusively Victorian-themed clothing, jewellery, and home decor; it promised 'an era of timeless charm, enduring quality, beauty and elegance … a breath of relief from this fast-paced world.' For nearly as long as we have had something like the modern world, we have had the people who created it offering us a relief from it. Given how tightly this tracks with most people's sense of nostalgia, it's no wonder it's been a common and effective marketing tactic. Quaker Oats was founded in 1877 and never actually run by Quakers; the company simply appropriated their reputation for honest dealing and used a representation of seventeenth-century American philosopher, colonist, and Quaker William Penn – he of Pennsylvania fame – as its logo, reportedly the country's oldest registered trademark for a cereal. Old Dutch cleansing powder, created from the leftover animal fat at

Chicago's Cudahy Packing plant in 1905, promised the fastidious Protestant work ethic of a beclogged sixteenth-century Dutch maid chasing down grease. Closer to our era, Baileys, the result of three years of intensive market research and product testing, debuted in 1974 with a name and logo reminiscent of a grand nineteenth-century London hotel, while Shinola resurrected a turn-of-the-century shoe polish brand name to give its watches and clothing an aura of age-old American industry and ingenuity. Shinola is one of the more successful examples of this rather naked nostalgia play, but it is far from alone: there are now auctions where aspiring entrepreneurs can buy the rights to retired product and corporate names. A 2010 auction in New York brought in close to $150,000 for names like defunct publisher Collier's, early plastic wrap staple Handi-Wrap, and classic stereo company Victrola. The latter is now used for an entire line of 'nostalgic Bluetooth record players' made to look like mid-century radios.

Where all these products promise some return to a distinct but only vaguely better era, personal nostalgia is agnostic toward the actual calendar and seeks only to remind you, the individual, of some better time in your life. Though it may come dressed in identifiable, period-specific fashion or form, the overriding goal is to prod you into reliving some intimate feeling and then let you intertwine the product into those warm fuzzies. It is undeniably a more delicate procedure – possibly getting easier with the intense personalization that web- and social-media-based advertising afford: what are Throwback Thursdays or Facebook year-in-reviews if not subtle marketing for their native platforms? – but is also a purer distillation of both marketing's purpose and nostalgia's practice. This tends to make the attempt to evoke personal nostalgia more resonant when it does hit, and seem more nakedly, incompetently manipulative when it doesn't. Freezer ads that try to evoke the warm security of being a kid in mom's kitchen are a fairly basic attempt at personal nostalgia, and by now a tried-and-true format: almost any advertisement or campaign that features children but isn't specifically for a children's product tends to lean heavy into nostalgia, whether that's a depiction of growing up with a dog fed with Iams kibble or Procter & Gamble showcasing moms who inspired their children to grow up to be Olympic athletes. Christmas campaigns are a gold mine for this, sliding into the slipstream of familial togetherness and tradition that already permeates the holiday. U.K. department store John Lewis, one of the undisputed champions of Yuletide advertising, leans hard into evoking memories of being a literal kid on Christmas Day in ads like 2009's 'The Feeling,' which featured children exploding with joy at getting adult gifts like coffee makers and laptops, or 2018's 'The Boy and the Piano,' which took a tour through Elton John's life (a nostalgia twofer), back to his first piano on Christmas morning.

In the later years of consumerist culture, personal nostalgia as sales tactic has been aided by the fact that many big brands are now old enough that they can indulge in nostalgia for themselves. There is no need, for instance, for McDonald's to try to associate itself with the warm, inclusive feeling of sitting down with the family to a home-cooked meal: for at least a couple generations of parents, there's a decent chance that gathering under the Golden Arches for McNuggets and fries is already a fountain of fond memories – or at least a fountain of memories that can be nudged toward fond with the right music cues and cutaway shots of fathers handing their daughters a nugget from across the ages. The undisputed champion of this sort of thing is Coca-Cola, which has the distinct advantage of being pervasive enough that it has created significant aspects of North American culture, most notably the iconic red-and-white image of Santa Claus. Coke is capable of inducing primal nostalgic feelings for its advertising alone, as evidenced by the biannual celebrations and recreations of its famous 'Hilltop' ad. It also pioneered taking self-reflexive consumerist nostalgia beyond mere marketing, letting it inspire entire products: leaning into the lesson it learned from the infamous New Coke debacle of the eighties – technically the new product rated better in taste tests, but it so offended nostalgic memories of what Coca-Cola should taste like that it bombed; in 1991 Coca-Cola reintroduced its classic 'contoured' green glass bottle. Despite being smaller than the standard aluminum can – and, a mere two years later, plastic bottle – it was a big enough hit that Coca-Cola has kept producing a small number of premium-priced bottles ever since. Its success provided the template for everything from Pepsi's occasional 'throwback' bottles to the likes of Volkswagen's New Beetle and Nintendo's Classic Edition consoles. Selling nostalgia is rarely more lucrative than when you own the trademark on the object people already use to define some part of what they once were.

This rose-tinted recursion is the logical end point of the inherent sympathy between consumerism and nostalgia, in more ways than one. There can't be a more perfect use of nostalgia in a consumerist society than this sort of closed loop, stoking the desire for more consumption by reminding people of what the original act of consumption meant to them. In constantly recycling the past, though, consumerism reveals nostalgia to be just another resource to be consumed. Memories, even good ones, are useless to consumerism until they can be dragged back and put to use in the name of creating that yearning that defines the consumerist impulse. Nostalgia, then, is the means by which consumerism colonizes the past, how it turns history into something that can be consumed, whether it's a collective experience like an era or a reborn turn-of-the-century stereo company or a personal experience like sharing a meal with a friend. Left entirely to its own devices, consumerist nostalgia would make both the past and nostalgia lesser; without countervailing forces to restock their power, they would become first subordinate and then ultimately meaningless. The past would never be left alone, continuously obscured by the present need to consume; nostalgia would be impossible, since nothing would ever really be left to yearning – nothing would ever really be out of reach.

As a more fundamental force, nostalgia is too big to really destroy. The consumerist tendency can certainly drain some objects or experiences of their nostalgia, making them common or graspable enough that the yearning disappears, but there will always be something else sufficiently out of reach to bring back that old familiar feeling. (Even if that might just be the subject of next year's advertisements.) Still, it may be worth remembering that the thing that gives nostalgia whatever power it has is that its yearning is ultimately unresolvable. Consumerism's meaning comes from hoping that one more thing will finally help you bridge the gap and get what you want; nostalgia's comes from learning there is peace in the void.

6

That's What She Said:
On the Future of Nostalgia

One of the bitterer truths that nostalgia helps us to deal with is the fact that we so rarely know when things are ending. Nearly all of the widely accepted momentous occasions of a life are those rare times when we are definitively, incontrovertibly aware that something is over: graduations and moving-away parties and retirements and funerals – admittedly it can be hard for a person to fully appreciate the importance of their own funeral – but even birthdays and anniversaries and weddings and births, too. Some of these events, of course, tend to be dominated more by the optimism of potential, but I don't think it's excessively cynical to suggest that we're able to really indulge the future precisely because we've had a chance to process and accept the fact that things are changing, that our school days or our pure independence or even just our twenties are definitively over. (And, of course, it's not at all rare for even the look-forward events to provoke nostalgia for the past that's about to be left behind.)

For all the big moments of finality and (ideally) transition, though, there are thousands of less obvious and often profoundly more meaningful endings that we realize only in retrospect, whether their finality creeps up on us across the ages or announces itself with thunderous realization. When was the last time your daughter fell asleep on your chest? The last time you had a drink with your best friend? The last time you ate the pasta at your favourite restaurant? The last time you petted your cat? The last time you felt like a kid? The last time a song made you cry? The last time you kissed your ex? The last time you hugged your old man? It's not just that we don't know while it's happening but that we literally can't until the experience is well and truly out of reach. We don't know what we've got until it's gone, and we don't even know when it will go.

The idea that things will go on forever is simple delusion on our part – all things pass, etc. – but as delusions go, it is surely among the most understandable, if not the most fundamentally necessary. The knowledge that life is fleeting is barely digestible in retrospect; in real time, it's debilitating. This is not even just poetic conjecture on my part. Insomuch as there are emerging fields in the world of nostalgia study, one of them is the idea of anticipatory nostalgia. This is, essentially, the realization that whatever you're currently experiencing will one day be something you look back on fondly. You might think that such a feeling would bring some deeper appreciation of the moment, some sort of odd time-loop Möbius strip of being present. And it can do that, on occasion, particularly on one of those happy occasions of transition we have had time to prepare for, like a wedding or birthday. But for the most part, becoming suddenly aware that a good experience is already in the process of becoming a memory mostly just makes us acutely sad. We may start thinking of other experiences that have also passed, or just be hit with the fundamentally transitory nature of all life's experience, but the end result is almost always a direct reversal of how nostalgia normally makes us feel: rather than perking up our present with pleasant reminders of what once was, it ruins it by reminding us that what is is rather rapidly becoming what was. (If you are looking for a bright side here: stop reflexively doing that. But also, there is no indication that the crash that comes from anticipatory nostalgia does anything to diminish regular old nostalgia down the road; you can have your cake, get sad about the fact you ate it, and much later remember how happy you were eating it, too.)

There does seem to be something particularly, self-defeatingly human about taking an emotion that has its main utility in easing our angst and finding a way to make it a new source of anxiety and frustration. Although the odder thing about anticipatory nostalgia is probably what it suggests about the role of nostalgia in our lives now. Nostalgia has managed to spill the banks of the past and is now capable, in a common enough way to be studiable, of flooding into our present moment; the fact that we regard the coming of nostalgia with something like dread also suggests that we see it as inevitable, a condition that can be fought or dismissed or, if we like, indulged, but never escaped. All things pass, and we will always wish we could have them back.

To what degree this is a wholly modern phenomenon is not entirely clear, although it's certainly not one that comes up terribly often in the earlier days of nostalgia; the closest we really get to it are concepts like Fred Davis's second-order nostalgia or Svetlana Boym's reflective nostalgia, but these are more explicitly about interrogating the act of looking back, not really what it might mean to anticipate looking back – a prospect that was evidently rare enough to hardly be worth exploring. At the risk of missing a chance to offer some grandiose theory, it seems most likely to be a fairly simple matter of cultural permeability: as the concept of nostalgia has become more of an everyday phenomenon, something frequently referenced and discussed, it seems only natural that this awareness will seep into the basic flavour of life. If anything, it may be the natural extension of Davis's and Boym's reflexive modes, not just interrogating the experience of nostalgia as it comes but cutting it off at the pass, as it were.

But then, of course, we are eliding the one truly fundamental question here, arguably the one that animates this entire book: why is it that nostalgia should have permeated our culture so thoroughly? We've explored the wheres and hows of it, and why it's a natural mode for some of the big forces of our society, but nothing becomes ubiquitous by force alone. You can't just plant an idea and hope it grows – you need fertile ground and careful tending. If the former is, as we explored in the first chapters, our natural tendency and desire to look back, the latter is the rapid expansion of media, in all its amorphously encompassing forms. We are not even capable of looking back with longing on a past that we are not aware of, and whatever else media allows us to do, it provides a deep and detailed (if not necessarily comprehensive) record of what came before; it is an awareness machine, sweeping up the past and allowing us to conveniently sift through the debris. Nostalgia, in this metaphor, would then be our feeling melancholy that something that was once useful is now junk (which is, at the very least, one of nostalgia's stronger flavours).

In less metaphorical terms, though, nostalgia is the inadvertent side effect of being exposed to our past. Its expansion across our psyche, to the point where it even plays into our conception of the future, fits rather perfectly with our awareness of both more and more past, and more pasts period. I'm not just trying to be rhetorically cute here: there is a kind of double-helix effect of recorded history, whereby not only are we recording events that then persist, but our continued familiarity with and expansion of forms of media start to give us different kinds of records, too. We can trace some aspect of human experience back to the oldest cave painting, a core of knowledge upon which the entirety of Twitter is now constantly adding its perspective: the expansion of both this core and the means by which we can add to it has gradually allowed us to encompass nearly the entirety of human experience, a past that is now both recorded and, most germanely, accessible in more or less real time.

Now, in fairness, there doesn't seem to be anything about mediated experience, even the expansive kind, that necessarily provokes nostalgia. Even if we have an infinite library, and even if we purposefully go looking through it from time to time, there's no reason why we should feel some longing to go back to it. Except that we, in the broad sense, do quite regularly seem to want to: knowledge of the past and desire for the past are, if not universally connected, then close enough that we haven't yet managed to create the former without getting at least a bit of the latter. If there is truth to the evergreen complaint that people seem to be more nostalgic than ever, it is almost certainly because we have never had more to be potentially nostalgic about, both in the sense of all human history and in the increasingly broad, though relatively recent, swaths of it that we've been able to document.

This isn't to suggest that this infinite library is some perfect repository of human memory: it is simply our own memory writ large, subject to both accidental and entirely purposeful elisions, erasures, and other losses, holes in the record that lead to holes in our understanding. But, as with the rest of the world, nostalgia runs on 'good enough.' It seems safe to say that, even if the loss of human experience and memory is incalculable – already many times larger than the actual record, and probably growing at at least the same rate as what's preserved – we have already well surpassed the point of having more than enough reference points to potentially yearn for. (Although there's a potential fun new avenue for nostalgia: a longing for pasts we're not even aware of.)

Because the march of both media and nostalgia has, until now, been almost entirely in one direction, it's tempting to imagine that we are on course to a world that will be utterly subsumed by nostalgia, where people gather just enough experience to have something to look back to, and retreat there indefinitely. Or, even worse, a *Ready Player One*–style hellscape where people are perfectly content to borrow someone else's nostalgia wholesale, hardly even interacting with the ongoing world long enough to form their own wistful memories.

This fear is, of course, not remotely unwarranted. There are a lot of ways to illustrate this, but something that seems particularly indicative to me is the American version of *The Office*. For those unaware, it is a serviceable and sometimes really quite funny remake of the more brutally cynical British TV show. It ran from 2005 to 2013, with solid if not world-breaking ratings – in the top hundred shows, but never in the top forty. Which is to say it was popular for long enough to give it some significant cultural heft, but it was also recent enough that you would not think it would be a particular object of nostalgic longing – it's barely had a chance to be missed. Despite this, one credible estimate suggests that this version of *The Office*, all by itself, accounted for more than 7 percent of all viewing among Netflix's American subscriber base in 2018. It works out to something like fifty-two billion minutes of the show in that one year alone: enough for every one of Netflix's sixty million or so American subscribers to have watched about two full seasons of *The Office* in 2018. Obviously that is not what is happening: even allowing for some first-timers or just first-time repeaters, there is some not-inconsequential segment of Netflix's audience that has made watching *The Office* something between an annual tradition and a daily routine.

Now, perhaps nostalgia is not purely responsible for every rewatching of a decent American sitcom, but it does seem fair to say that, by the time you can recite the punchlines of a comedy – particularly a seventy-hour-comedy – the memory of laughter is driving at least as much enjoyment as whatever you might be discovering. And *The Office*, especially on a platform like Netflix, is almost perfectly suited to capturing a very particular kind of nostalgic longing. Being a tech platform, Netflix draws an audience that skews a bit young – in fact, just slightly older than the teens and early-twenties demographic who were among *The Office*'s biggest fans during its initial run. These original fans are now in the period of early-life turmoil – graduating school, starting careers and families, being confronted by serious questions about Who You Are – that makes people prone to nostalgia. The show's setting is exactly the kind of slightly glossy version of their current day-to-day drudgery – everyone's just a bit more quirky, a bit more clever, a bit more attractive – that is both eminently relatable and a nice escape from another day of it. And, if you already have a Netflix subscription, and especially if you have already watched *The Office*, watching it again is as easy as opening your laptop, or even just doing nothing and letting the autoplay run. Given the smallest emotional hook – this beloved show from my youth might even be more relevant to me today! – you can end up in an endless loop, where a show that never managed to be among the top forty most popular shows while it was is being created is now the de facto cornerstone for the most important cultural platform of the last decade. (And if online *Office* fandom is any indication, an even bigger portion of some people's personalities.)

Whatever unique quirks make *The Office* the undisputed champion of the rewatch, though, it is hardly alone: the second-most popular show in 2018 was the two-decade-old *Friends*, which accounted for a full 4 percent of all Netflix watching – and, though I'm just guessing here, a similar percentage of BuzzFeed content, too. And, of course, the expansive, easily accessible archive has always been one of the internet's key promises. Way back in 2006, when *The Office* was still just a mere knock-off, *Wired* editor-in-chief Chris Anderson wrote about the promise of the Long Tail. The basic idea is that, where analogue shops were hamstrung by the need to physically stock things, which typically limited the availability of anything but the widest-selling, block-buster-type products, online businesses, free of physical necessities, could find bigger profits in offering many more niche products – individually they weren't big sellers, but taken together they accounted for more sales overall than the few big hits. The prime example of this strategy was Amazon, which at the time was able to offer many more books than any individual retailer (and also seriously undercut any other retailer, which was perhaps an underexplored aspect of its success in this conception); the degree to which optimism about the potential for the Long Tail was warranted probably depends on your current opinion of Amazon's business model.

If there ever was a meaningful difference between cultural consumption and commerce, the internet has thoroughly flattened it. And in any case, the potential implications for nostalgia are the same, whether your concern is selling books or reading them: what has been produced will always dwarf what's currently being produced. If the only thing that was preventing us from diving thoroughly into the past was basic accessibility, then the only thing that might keep us exploring the current would be … curiosity? Novelty? Humanity's insatiable wanderlust? Whatever it is, it is some intangible quality that will be set against the powerful comforts of nostalgia, of bathing in an emotional state that expressly makes us feel like healthy, well-adjusted, whole people.

But even assuming that our entertainment and leisure time will be spent consuming cultural artifacts is at best narrow-minded and at worst hopelessly quaint. Our increasing mediation has also given us unprecedented access to our personal memories, a realm of experience that multiplies the potency of nostalgia many times. One could argue that the dominant mode of public media experience even now is just a series of overlapping personal narratives, the cascade of opinions and selfies and advice posts and multi-tagged pictures of dinner occupying as much of our ongoing attention as any of the things they are reacting to, or are within, or are shaded by. But even if a distinction between these things is too knotty to sort out – is a meme about how some aspect of your life is just like that scene from *The Office* more about your life or more about *The Office*? – the potential to relive purely personal experience alone has never been greater. Forget even the not-yet-digitized photo albums and waiting-to-be-converted VHS tapes of birthday celebrations lurking in basements, destined to be sorted through when their inadvertent archivists die: the iPhone was released in 2007, which would imply there is at least one twelve-year-old in the world who could probably stitch together an animation of their every waking moment with nothing more than the right iCloud passwords. And these are just the intentionally documented moments: depending on how particular you are about privacy settings, Google has a nearly up-to-the-minute record of your location, anything you've ever been curious enough to ask it, and maybe all of your personal correspondence from roughly the same time frame, available at a click.

At a glance, this infinite personal archive might seem like something of an existential threat to nostalgia. Facts about our lives are now verifiable with an ease that goes well beyond rooting through old photo albums; if we're able not just to think fondly on past experiences but to call up a reasonable simulacrum, it might leave us more suspicious of the nostalgic impulse, or perhaps even short-circuit the nostalgia process entirely, leaving us with just the picture of memories, not the warm and fuzzy feelings of them. This doesn't seem to be the case, though. For starters, being able to double-check our memories rarely does anything to affect our feeling of them, and nostalgia seems to be too automatic a process to erase in this way: just as we can't help checking out potential new partners even after going through a terrible breakup, evidence of a faulty memory doesn't do much to prevent our subconscious from subtly altering our memories anyway. Besides, even this personal cornucopia is still severely hamstrung by our current media technologies: no photo captures what we were feeling or thinking, which is where the real meat of the meaning of our memories resides. Barring an incorruptible implant in our frontal cortex, technology that gives us more memory only seems to give us more potential for nostalgia.

This potential will only be further realized as our ability to recreate our pasts gets deeper and more sophisticated. What might happen when we're able not just to go back and read our old love e-mails or watch the video of our children taking their first steps but to immerse ourselves in some digital simulacrum, actually seem to experience it again, albeit with slightly older senses? Digital artist Sarah Rothberg offered a glimpse of what this might look like with her project *Memory/Place: My House*, an Oculus Rift–based art exhibit that allowed viewers to travel through a recreated version of her childhood home. Moving through it would trigger home videos shot by her father, superimposed over the digital stand-ins of the various rooms. Though only the most drug-addled would mistake it for anything but an artificial experience, Rothberg did report that moving through the simulation had curious side effects, beyond just giving her a chance to relive memories: it triggered new memories that merely poring over videos and photos had not – one of the most prominent for her was a recollection of a loose floorboard in the hallway. This would suggest the possibility that more immersive formats of nostalgia would not just offer the usual comforts in 3-D but might build on themselves, letting us plumb new depths of memory or perhaps even giving us a chance to synthesize the nostalgic appeal of return with the rush of novelty, providing something like a new experience wrapped in the comforting appeal of one we already know and love. (Kind of like watching a TV show multiple times.) And if these suddenly deeper recollections have the potential to ruin our most cherished personal memories – heaven forbid we suddenly remember that Mom and Dad actually fought their way through our ninth birthday – we could always limit this to our cultural artifacts: you may have seen *The Office* fifteen times through, but you haven't seen it from the perspective of Michael Scott.

On the note of perspective, though: if there is an upper limit on the technological potential for the relentless expansion of nostalgia, it will be between being lightly prodded to remember something from our past and tricking ourselves (or being tricked) into thinking we are fully experiencing these things again. Call it something like an internal uncanny valley, where a situation is still recognizably a memory we are accessing, and not just a fully immersive, recreated experience. Assuming the latter is even theoretically possible, we are entering Matrix territory; even if we ignored the full terrain of reality-bending simulation and limited it to simply the idea of recreating experiences from our past, we would not really be instilling a yearning: we would, for all intents and purposes, be transporting ourselves back there. Nostalgia as we understand it would be, if not entirely redundant, at least robbed of its impossibility, and as such of any real meaning – it would become something more like hunger, or lust, an itch to be scratched.

I don't think we need to get into far-future sci-fi-ish predictions, though, to see the point where nostalgia might be bled of its meaning. Because for all the potential we have created for nostalgia – for all that the constant evolution of media has seemed to create conditions where nostalgia is not just inevitable but perhaps even threatening to become one of the dominant modes of interacting with the world – there is also something about our current world that seems like a threat to nostalgia. If it is not a fully existential threat, it is one that seems destined to flatten nostalgia into an experience with no real potency – into something that retains its basic shape, with none of the weight or depth.

The root of the issue, I think, is that the infinite library we have built has reached its breadth not because we were trying to create a repository of human knowledge but because we have a fanatical devotion to continuing to build. To the extent that our modern modes of media can be said to have a goal, it is not record-keeping, nor dissemination, nor even appreciation; it is simple engagement with the media itself, simple attention to everything it is consuming and extruding. We are an infinite number of monkeys, but the purpose is not Shakespeare; it is to keep the typewriter industry afloat. (Or maybe, if you want to be slightly less cynical about it, to fill the air with the sounds of typewriters.)

Some of this is baked into the very nature of our new media platforms themselves. Though they seem to offer some kind of permanent record of the world – at least so long as the servers are still running or no one has accidentally deleted all the things on them – the platforms are in a constant state of evolution, one that has the effect of obliterating any past version of itself.

Most forms of our media have remained fundamentally consistent since their invention, and our experience of them has followed suit. Certainly, it is easier to create books with desktop publishing software and digital printers than with a team of monks, and yes, the automatic save-your-place features of a cross-platform e-reader are a little more convenient than a bookmark. But these are relatively minor tweaks to the experience of producing a physical book that someone then grabs, sits down, and pores over. Some of our more recent media technologies have maybe gone through some more substantive changes to our experience of them – there is probably a meaningful difference between sitting in a room full of strangers to watch the illusion of movement on film and being able to watch streaming digital video in your own private bubble with headphones while on the subway, or playing a video game on a stand-up arcade machine versus playing it in an emulated version on your laptop (Twin Galaxies, the world's authority on video game high scores, is particular about that one, for instance). But ultimately we are still just reading or watching or listening or playing. Even if these are different enough to be considered different mediums, the invention of e-books or hi-def video did not coincide with the mass destruction of every hand-bound volume or strip of celluloid. For now, at least, they're still available to us, should we want them.

By contrast, the internet is not just extremely fungible, it is, after shorter and shorter intervals, impossible to recreate in anything but an emptily aesthetic sense. You see this in our futile attempts to archive it: websites like Version History, which tracks the changing facades of notable sites like Amazon, Google, the *New York Times,* and YouTube, can offer little more than screenshots – a collection of slightly uncanny fonts, aged logos, and unfamiliar arrangements all that remains of what were once fully interactive environments that pushed you around the web. In certain instances, people have managed to create walled gardens of earlier versions of the internet, something like video game emulators for dicking around online circa 2009. The most famous of these is the Internet Archive's Wayback Machine, which is capable of creating cached versions of websites, quite regularly maintaining almost all the images and formatting of a regular website, as well as links that frequently work, taking you to other cached versions of other websites. The illusion tends to fall apart the instant you try to do anything other than merely look at them, but if your experience of the internet is limited to checking news sites or Wikipedia – no comments or edits – it's perhaps close enough.

The root cause of the simulation's failure is interactivity: being able to not just actively create but engage with and subtly alter the content of the entire format is not just a feature of the internet, it is the entire point – if anything, the fact that some sort of archive is left over is just happy coincidence. We see this best when we consider social media, which feels in many ways like the distilled purpose and promise of the internet, grim as that may be.

Compared to the interface of Facebook or Twitter or Instagram (or TikTok or whatever else has exploded in the time between this writing and your reading) that we are greeted by every time we open their apps, any archive the Wayback

Machine offers is resplendently dead, words and images behind a glass we can't zoom into or double-tap on. This irrevocability isn't, of course, immediately obvious to us, because another essential aspect of these forms of media is amorphous evolution, incorporating their changes in such a way that it becomes almost impossible to look back and see that anything has changed.

On Instagram, for instance, your profile page handily archives every picture you have ever posted to the service, which all of your friends and possibly the rest of the public can see (unless you choose to delete the posts, but that's a choice that goes beyond the baseline construction of the service). In a sense, these are still part of what you might call current Instagram: they can still be viewed, even liked and commented on, although not even Instagram's desperate engagement algorithm will automatically resurface them to other people (and, generally speaking, interacting with anything more than about two weeks old is seen as a major social faux pas for users of all stripes). And yet their context has been warped, drastically, repeatedly, and, from the vantage point of today – or even of just someone who signed up to Instagram a little later than you – invisibly. In simply looking through someone's old photos, you cannot meaningfully recreate the context they were created in: this batch was done when there were only a half-dozen kinds of filters, this before you could post multiple pictures at the same time; these existed before you could publicize them with hashtags, these before you could tag friends, these when Instagram's feed was still organized chronologically, these before it introduced Stories; these had more likes and comments before half of my friends deleted their accounts; and on and on and on.

These aren't just garden-variety shifts in societal norms or cultural understandings that require us to do a bit of digging to understand, either; this isn't 'Blurry pictures of water lilies were revolutionary in a world of realism' or 'Oh, to get this joke you have to know that Shakespeare was making a reference to the Duke of Motherfordshire, who was a famous lush.' Nor are these a matter of incorporating new techniques or abilities within an extant medium, like inventing the interrobang, or cutting two strips of film together. These are fundamental changes to how and why things are created, not just received, within the medium itself, the rules and parameters of how we engage with this thing called Instagram altered – with the change effectively erased – in less than a decade of its existence.

And an even more crucial distinction here is that, even if we could reverse all these changes and return to the original platform, or maybe even just the version of it that was running when this particular image was taken, we are still not meaningfully recreating the platform as it existed then – we are just looking at a better museum exhibit. To actually experience Instagram as Instagram 2011 – or Facebook as Facebook 2006, or Twitter, etc. – to capture the expansiveness and unpredictability and genuine interactivity of the whole, we would effectively need to revert the entire world back to the same platform (which would make all the other iterations just as meaningless). Which is to say, of course, that we can't. Which makes these forms of media, unique among medias, powerfully resistant to nostalgia: we can revisit a book or a film or a personal photograph, and we can sort of revisit a tweet or an instagram, but we can never really revisit Instagram as such – it will always be whatever the latest version of Instagram is, always have taken the place of itself. It's hard for us to remember something that doesn't leave any palpable trace, and impossible to be nostalgic for something we don't remember.

Now, perhaps this doesn't really matter: perhaps in the same way that social media can be a digital analogue for offline experiences – what it's like to share an opinion over the dinner table, or show someone a photo – it will be a conduit for memory, the place where we store the records of the things we want to look back on. This is sort of true of any broad media category: books haven't changed, but it's not as if we're ever really nostalgic for the *concept* of books – it's a specific one, in the same way that maybe it will be a specific post or, more accurately, the specific experience that post was depicting. There is an extent to which the internet is a bunch of concepts and forces that have already existed, just faster and more concentrated in a way that can seem frightening, and it could be that the social media platform we are sharing these things on will ultimately be as important as the pen we used to write our journal with, memory/ nostalgia-wise: mostly forgotten.

If so, though, it seems to me that will happen only if we fundamentally change our relationship to these platforms. As it stands now, they are not just the latest form of media, another option in our quiver of ways to interact with the world; they are something like the bedrock of our understanding of the world, their effects spreading out even to people who try not to engage with them. And their fundamental resistance to a sort of self-reflexive nostalgia seems to be mirrored in how we use them and how they use us.

The first half of the equation comes in the form of what these media platforms seem to do to our identity. Jaron Lanier lays out these ideas best in his books *You Are Not a Gadget* and *Ten Arguments for Deleting Your Social Media Accounts Right Now*, the gist of which is that social media – partly by design and partly in practice – is a tool for distilling the breadth of human experience into something like commercially useful synecdoches, atomizing our sense of self into its most saleable qualities. The most obvious example of this is something like LinkedIn, where your professional history becomes you; if the nakedness of LinkedIn's purpose makes it easier to separate out this particular personal avatar from the expanse of the real thing – You Are Not a Resumé – most of the less purposeful social media platforms are much better at fuzzing the distinction. Not only is their overarching personality filter harder to immediately grasp – are you any more than the sum of things you find visually interesting, like Instagram assumes? – many of them are better at sorting you within themselves, going well beyond 'job-seekers in a particular city' into overlapping demographic slices that dictate the entirety of your experience on these platforms.

There is a degree to which we can resist this flattening of our identity: not everyone is an influencer, and most people are dimly aware or at least occasionally reminded that authenticity is usually something performed on social media, not a necessary corollary (though I'm not sure how often this seeps all the way down into awareness of their own online activities). But the idea that mass numbers of people could spend ever-expanding amounts of time interacting with platforms where the default setting is to pigeonhole you, without ever having that bleed over into their self-conception, seems hopelessly optimistic. We are what we tell ourselves we are, but that is plainly influenced by what we are told we are – and some of our most pervasive (and meaningful) interactions are telling us that we are indeed gadgets of some sort or another. (And this doesn't even get into the effects such perceptions might have on people who did not even have a chance to form meaningful senses of self before plugging into a half-dozen different social medias, the effects of which we're only just beginning to feel.)

Of course, this effect on our identity is not just a side effect of how these forms have been built. Nearly all social media platforms – and you can easily extend this to any endeavour that is making its nut via the internet – are very expressly engagement machines, designed to draw in as much of our attention as we are willing to give them. Our demographic profile is a road map of how to hook us, and as such is ruthlessly exploited whenever it keeps us scrolling, clicking, and coming back. But while the rush for engagement reinforces tight parameters on our identity, it also creates its own set of problems related to its constant, habitual use.

When people tend to talk about what the internet is doing to our memory, they tend to fall into the Google trap – the realization that surely every one of us has had that the instant our Wi-Fi or cellphone data goes away, so too does our ability to remember everything from who starred in *The Sopranos* to the birthdays of most of our loved ones or what it is we're doing next weekend. If this is personally disconcerting, though, this kind of external memory has been around since writing, more or less, and most research suggests that there is not anything substantially different between the way we access information online and the way we would use, say, a Rolodex: our brain is efficient, good at storing what it really needs and knowing how to find the rest, and even if the internet disappeared tomorrow, we would be able to relearn some functional memory skills.

The bigger challenge to our memories comes from the fact that much of social media – and again, the internet writ large – is essentially designed to short-circuit our conscious, active awareness of what's going on around us, which tends to obliterate our ability to form much in the way of meaningful memories at all. The popular metaphor at this moment is gambling: in the same way that the low-level anxiety and occasional rushes of variable reward can cause (mostly problem) gamblers to lose vast swaths of time, the endless scroll of a social media feed – algorithmically attuned to our interests, constantly refreshable and offering almost random dollops of strong emotional reaction or other encouragements to keep looking and posting – seems to just obliterate long stretches of time, lulling us into a sort of trance with no beginning or end.

Some of this is unintentional, at least: for whatever reason, digital things do not seem to promote memory in the same way physical things do. Taking a digital picture, for instance, seems to reduce people's memory of whatever it was they snapped, while printed-out pictures are quite useful memory objects. This might just be because the endless stream of digital photos puts them in the category of things we need to know how to find, not things we need to know. But most of it is intentional: awareness of how long you've been doing something will lead you to question why you're doing it, and possibly even stop – the last thing any social media platform wants. The fact that older versions of most social media platforms are utterly impossible to access today is a perfect expression of what the platforms want: to provide a sense of inevitability, to expand into everything, to create an experience that is never going away, and never wasn't there, exactly as it is now.

Throwing an increasingly fractured or limited self into an everlasting now would seem, on the surface, like a recipe to kill nostalgia entirely. It is a world where there is almost nothing meaningful to remember, and where even that is being overwhelmed by a constant flood of new things designed to capture your attention. But this might be an ideal breeding ground for nostalgia, albeit a nostalgia that isn't a lot more than one in a long stream of dopamine hits. Things that break down identity are perfect incubators for nostalgic feeling – it is precisely when we feel compelled to solidify some sense of self that we are most nostalgic. In the constant stream, nostalgia also has the advantage of being a reliably powerful hit of emotion, a reward to be doled out infrequently but consequentially.

This cycle alone would seem to explain at least part of why nostalgia-influenced content – our endless parade of anniversaries, reappraisals, and throwbacks – is such an effective strategy for any variety of online enterprises. The business model demands an identity that is fractured, and it needs you to be not only okay with that fact but eager to explore it further and further. Enter nostalgia, which seems help you heal your identity and can be revisited again and again. Excitement, happiness, anger, laughter – plenty of other sources of strong feeling at least require some sense of novelty, something new to prod these feelings at something like the same level. Nostalgia is always just as comforting, because it is always drawing us back to ourselves. Nostalgia is the selfie of subject matter.

What sort of nostalgia is this, though? Its restorative powers would seem to be, if not entirely elusive, at least easy to reset, lasting no longer than the next bit of content, which by its nature needs to siphon you off again. The mere fact that many social media networks make a point of resurfacing your old posts, mining their own most obvious vein of nostalgia, means they think it is a good way of keeping you around; this is nostalgia as gasoline, something you can use to fill your sense of self just enough so that you keep engaging and don't get too distressed or depressed that you lose the will to log on. It's certainly the same mechanism, but it feels like one that has been reduced to a stimulus response, a reflex. Something that was once so profoundly disconcerting it was deemed pathological has been rendered about as harmless as a sneeze, as easily triggered and as easily cured, or, anyway, dismissed until we want or need it again.

It's entirely possible that that's all nostalgia ever was, that perhaps we just lacked the knowledge and infrastructure to really boil it down to its most effective essence, or were so caught up in its effects that we never bothered to notice how merely reflexive it was. If this is true, it's hard to conceive of nostalgia as a truly meaningful force in our lives without falling into a bit of a nostalgia trap. Perhaps the most hard-headed way we could frame this would be that who or what we are is always far more open a question than we really want to admit, and that our underlying, unbearable uncertainty absolutely requires an easily accessible, almost inexhaustible resource, something that springs up almost automatically whenever a fuzzy sense of self threatens to overwhelm us. Ultimately, all we are is the memory of ourselves – it would make sense that we would find a way to jump-start our most important memories, and that this tendency would go into hyperdrive as soon as we had access to any memory we could want.

If there is something lost in this sort of easily exploitable materialist conception of nostalgia, though, it is nostalgia's confounding impossibility, its yearning for something that can't be. Identity solidification might be nostalgia's most useful function, but it's hardly the only way we can pull that off: most directly, we could just go out and start doing things, becoming, or, anyway, just continuing to be what it is we think we are. Nostalgia has not just hung around but imposed itself more on our consciousness because the modern flood of memory is also close to another of life's profundities, another reality that we are loath to admit, and one we certainly don't indulge on social media as fervently: the fact that, soon enough, we won't be around anymore.

Naturally, nostalgia is as absurd as any attempt to really reckon with death: ultimately our memories will fade just as surely as the past they're recalling, and the dream that things might happen again, the absolutely overwhelming yearning to be back in that time, in that place, is the same as the one that assumes we will continue on indefinitely. At least in nostalgia's case, we are clinging to something that has happened before.

Or that we imagine has happened before. Though we give it a halo of fact, nostalgia has a funny relationship with authenticity. It is plainly not an authentic accounting of what has happened – which we know, distantly, even when we're in the grips of it. All the same, it's one of the truer feelings we can have; it makes us feel, after all, like ourselves. This feeling is about all the defence we can muster against the end, inadequate as it may be: the idea not just that we existed, but were knowable, sensible, had some kind of arc or meaning – even if it never extended much beyond our own head.

It is not much, maybe, but it is the best we can do, under the circumstances. Even if it's reduced to some threadbare content strategy, our nostalgia is something that is unequivocally ours; it won't be possible to miss it when it's gone.

Conclusion:
The Memory of Ourselves

Our impending death seems like the natural place to end a discussion of nostalgia. Nostalgia is, in its way, the dream that we can give death a little bit less bite, that not everything will crumble into mere memory, that we can have things back. For that reason, at least from where I sit, it is just as inevitable as death. The cost of our awareness of mortality is the desire to be free of it; the cost of our memory is the desire to go back to what we remember. We do that because we think the times we remember were simpler or better or more true, maybe, but we also do it because we can't help ourselves.

There is something perversely and wonderfully human about wanting to go back being as inevitable as being pulled forward. I think part of the reason I was drawn to writing about nostalgia is that it's an exemplary condition, an idea that speaks directly to our limitations, to our dizzying irrationality, to our continued inability to fit ourselves into a sensible shape. If there is a danger in celebrating that side of ourselves, there may be a greater danger in ignoring it: we have an incredible ability to attribute collective follies exclusively to other individuals, and I would hope that if you got nothing else from this book, you were at least occasionally reminded of how fragile and haphazard a thing you really are.

Better thinkers than I have described nostalgia as an acutely modern condition. They are probably right, although I do think it's important to underline that that's because so much of our modern world is shaped to help us indulge nostalgia, not because it hasn't always been a part of us. The root of this push is not so much alienation or globalization as it is individualism, the literally Romantic idea not only that we have a self, but that realizing it and living true to it is our highest purpose. We are more nostalgic now because nostalgia helps us to make sense of ourselves: we are what we remember we are, and nostalgia helps us remember what we want to be.

Because of the way nostalgia intertwines with our sense of self, it will always be ripe for exploitation. This is why something that seems like such a natural wrench in the gears of progress has been more often turned into grease: knowing ourselves is such messy business that we are always eager to let someone else figure it out for us, even if they're only doing it so they can sell us gas. As much as I think some of our base-level unease with nostalgia stems from what it reveals about how foggy our self-perception really is, the more cynical side of me recognizes our distrust as a healthy natural defence. Because it is comforting, because it is essential, because it is inevitable, nostalgia will always be an easy way in. If I think that maybe we should be less suspicious of our own nostalgic impulses, we could stand to be far more suspicious of anyone who tries to indulge them for us.

There will only be more opportunity for nostalgic indulgence of all kinds in the years ahead. Some of that is because the world's own future seems ever more in doubt; naturally our past will seem to offer either more clarity or more comfort, a way to deal with it or a way to retreat from it. But even beyond that, as our experience of the world becomes increasingly mediated, the dissonance of our identity and the malleability of our memory only become more apparent. Nostalgia could help us reconcile these forces, could help us find the meaning in the mess crucial for anything like a satisfying life; it could also just be another vector for optimization, one of an infinite number of strings that gets pulled to make a flattened and disassociated way of being feel more like the real thing.

I would not have written a book about our yearning for our history if I had any confidence in my ability to predict the future. The most that can be said is that, presuming we survive, someone somewhere will look back and wish they could do it again.

Works Cited

Anderson, Chris. *The Long Tail: Why the Future of Business Is Selling Less of More.* New York: Hyperion Books, 2006.

Back to the Future. Directed by Robert Zemeckis. Universal City: Universal Pictures, 1985.

Boym, Svetlana. *The Future of Nostalgia.* New York: Basic Books, 2001.

Campbell, Colin. *The Romantic Ethic and the Spirit of Modern Consumerism.* New Jersey: Blackwell Publishing, 1987.

Cline, Earnest. *Ready Player One.* New York: Penguin Random House, 2011.

Davis, Fred. *Yearning for Yesterday.* New York: Free Press, 1979.

Hobsbawm, Eric, and Terence Ranger, eds. *The Invention of Tradition.* Cambridge: Cambridge University Press, 2012.

Illbruck, Helmut. *Nostalgia: Origins and Ends of an Unenlightened Disease.* Evanston: Northwestern University Press, 2012.

Judt, Tony. 'The Past Is Another Country: Myth and Memory in Postwar Europe.' *Daedalus* 121, no. 4 (1992).

Lanier, Jaron. *You Are Not a Gadget.* New York: Alfred A. Knopf, 2010.

———. *Ten Arguments for Deleting Your Social Media Accounts Right Now.* New York: Macmillan, 2018.

Lethem, Jonathan. *The Ecstasy of Influence: Nonfictions, Etc.* New York: Doubleday, 2011.

Marinetti, F. T. *Manifesto del Futurismo.* Original printing: Milan 1909.

Noether, Emiliana. 'The Seeds of Italian Nationalism, 1700-1815.' *The American Historical Review* 57, no. 2 (1952): 438–39.

Packard, Vance. *The Hidden Persuaders.* Philadelphia: D. McKay Co., 1957.

———. *The Waste Makers.* Philadelphia: D. McKay Co., 1960.

Poggioli, Renato. *The Theory of the Avant-Garde.* Cambridge: Harvard University Press, 1981.

Proust, Marcel. *À la recherche du temps perdu.* Paris: Éditions Grasset, 1913–27.

Reynolds, Simon. *Retromania: Pop Culture's Addiction to Its Own Past.* London: Faber & Faber, 2010.

Rousseau, Jean-Jacques. 'Considerations on the Government of Poland.' In *Rousseau: The Social Contract and Other Later Political Writings,* 2nd ed., Ed. Victor Gourevitch. Cambridge Texts in the History of Political Thought. Cambridge: Cambridge University Press, 2018. doi:10.1017/9781316584606.003.

Routledge, Clay. *Nostalgia: A Psychological Resource.* Abingdon: Routledge, 2016.

The Star Wars Saga. Lucasfilm.

Stranger Things. Netflix. 2016–19.

Acknowledgements

I would like to thank libraries in general, and the Toronto Reference and University of Alberta Rutherford libraries in particular. Their (nearly) infinite archives make nostalgia possible, and their calm makes writing possible.

I would like to thank the very smart and thoughtful editors who have an even better claim on making writing possible. Thank you, Emily Keeler, for shaping the book; Alana Wilcox for shepherding it; and Peter Norman for saving me from my tics, insomuch as that is possible.

Thank you to all of the people who listened to me while I tried to explain some part of this book or why I was writing it. Naturally, I don't remember all of you, but I hope you look back on those conversations fondly.

And, of course, thank you to Nicki, who besides keeping our daughter alive through this process has also been a font of good ideas and has handled the anxieties and orneriness of a writer with more grace than any marriage vow could have demanded. I can honestly say, from the deepest part of myself, go Margot go.

David Berry is a writer and cultural critic in Edmonton. His work has appeared in the *Globe and Mail, Hazlitt, Toronto Life*, and elsewhere, and he was an arts and culture columnist for the *National Post* for five years. This is his first book.

Typeset in Albertina

Printed at the old Coach House on bpNichol Lane in Toronto, Ontario, on Rolland Opaque Natural paper, which was manufactured, acid-free, in Saint-Jérôme, Quebec, from 50 percent recycled paper, and it was printed with vegetable-based ink on a 1972 Heidelberg KORD offset litho press. Its pages were folded on a Baumfolder, gathered by hand, bound on a Sulby Auto-Minabinda, and trimmed on a Polar single-knife cutter.

Seen through the press by Alana Wilcox
Acquired by Emily Keeler
Edited by Peter Norman
Cover by Raymond Biesinger
Author photo by Jessica Fern Facette

Coach House Books
80 bpNichol Lane
Toronto ON M5S 3J4
Canada

416 979 2217
800 367 6360

mail@chbooks.com
www.chbooks.com